P9-DXN-384

Jackie Robinson

Young Sports Trailblazer

Illustrated by Meryl Henderson

Jackie Robinson

Young Sports Trailblazer

by Herb Dunn

ALADDIN PAPERBACKS

If you purchased this book without a cover you should be aware that this book is stolen property. It was reported as "unsold and destroyed" to the publisher and neither the author nor the publisher has received any payment for this "stripped book."

First Aladdin Paperbacks edition March 1999

Text copyright © 1999 by Dan Gutman
Illustrations copyright © 1999 by Meryl Henderson

Aladdin Paperbacks
An imprint of Simon & Schuster Children's Publishing Division
1230 Avenue of the Americas
New York, NY 10020

All rights reserved, including the right of reproduction in whole or in part in any form.
The text for this book was set in New Caledonia
The illustrations were rendered in pen and ink with wash.
Printed and bound in the United States of America
10 9 8 7 6 5 4 3 2 1

Library of Congress Cataloging-in-Publication Data
Herb Dunn.
Jackie Robinson : young sports trailblazer / by Herb Dunn ;
illustrated by Meryl Henderson. — 1st Aladdin Paperbacks ed.
p. cm. — (Childhood of famous Americans series)
Includes bibliographical references (p. 9).
Summary: A biography emphasizing the childhood of the baseball legend who became the first African American to play Major League baseball.
ISBN 0-689-87840-0 (pbk.)
1. Robinson, Jackie, 1919–1972—Juvenile literature. 2. Baseball players—United States—Biography—Juvenile literature.
[1. Robinson, Jackie, 1919–1972. 2. Baseball players. 3. Afro-Americans—Biography.]
I. Henderson, Meryl, ill. II. Title. III. Series.
GV865.R6G88 1999
796.357'092—dc21 [b] 98-45623
CIP AC

Illustrations

Contents

ACKNOWLEDGMENT

The information in this book was gathered by reading many previous books about Jackie Robinson. Particularly helpful were: *Jackie Robinson: A Life Remembered*, by Maury Allen; *The Jackie Robinson Reader*, edited by Jules Tygiel; *Jackie Robinson: A Biography*, by Arnold Rampersad; and Jackie Robinson's autobiography, *I Never Had It Made*.

"It took an intelligent man to understand the challenge–
it took a man of great moral courage to accept it and see it through.

He was both."

– BRANCH RICKEY,
FORMER DODGER PRESIDENT
ON JACKIE ROBINSON

THE DODGERS PROUDLY SALUTE
THE LIFE OF JACKIE ROBINSON.

Dodgers™

dodgers.com

DodgeR Coca-Cola FaMiLY PacK

4 tickets + 4 Dodger Dogs + 4 Cokes + 1 parking pass = $48

EVERY WEDNESDAY AND SUNDAY HOME GAME!

7 DAY ADVANCE PURCHASE REQUIRED TO RECEIVE PARKING PASS

Dodgers

Call 323-224-1-HIT

dodgers.com

Jackie Robinson

Young Sports Trailblazer

Fighting Back

Sweep . . . sweep . . . sweep . . .

Eight-year-old Jackie Robinson brushed the big broom across the sidewalk in front of his little house on Pepper Street in Pasadena, California. All five of the Robinson children had a job they had to do every day. Jackie's job was to keep the sidewalk spotless.

It wasn't a hard job. In fact, Jackie was having fun. He pretended that his broom was a hockey stick, and he fired a slap shot into an imaginary net. Whack! The dirt flew into the street. Then he pretended his broom was a golf club, and he drove a tee shot far down an imaginary fairway. Wham!

It was October 1927. Jackie had heard about a famous baseball player named Babe Ruth who hit an amazing sixty home runs that season. Nobody had *ever* done that before. Jackie pretended his broom was a baseball bat, and he cracked a home run over an imaginary center-field fence. *Smash!* The dirt went flying off the sidewalk.

It was a joyful time. Jackie was lost in his thoughts and fantasies, imagining that he was a famous athlete.

Suddenly, a girl about Jackie's age came out of her house down the street. She saw Jackie. Her face immediately twisted up into a scowl and she spat out just one word. "Nigger!"

With that one word, Jackie's mood changed instantly. The happiness he had been feeling washed away from him. It was replaced by anger, a deep anger that began to well up inside him.

Jackie had heard the word before, but nobody had ever said it to *him*. He knew it was a bad word. It was a word that some white people would use against people who looked like Jackie—people who had dark skin.

"That girl doesn't even know me," Jackie thought to himself as he stared at her. "We never talked. Why is she calling me names? How can she possibly dislike me so much?"

Jackie was too young to understand how people of different races and ethnic groups sometimes don't get along together. It didn't make sense to him. People were just *people*. Why should somebody's skin color have anything to do with the kind of person he or she was? But the girl had made him very mad, and he wanted to make her mad right back.

He remembered something his older brother Frank once told him. Frank said that back in Georgia, where the Robinsons used to live, the worst thing you could call a white person was "cracker."

"Cracker!" Jackie yelled at the girl. She ran back into her house and slammed the door.

Jackie went back to his sidewalk sweeping and forgot about the girl. He pretended that his broom was a tennis racquet, and he smacked a backhand across an imaginary court. *Slam!*

At that moment a rock whizzed past Jackie's head. It smacked into the tree behind him with a thud. Jackie stiffened. He spun around to see where the rock might have come from. A man was standing in front of the girl's house. He was staring at Jackie. "It must be her father," Jackie thought.

"Hey, you!" the man yelled. "Are you bothering my daughter?"

Jackie didn't answer. He knew that a black person who talked disrespectfully to a white person could be hurt—or even worse. He just looked at the man, trying to decide what to do next.

"I'm talking to *you*, boy!" the man

hollered, picking up another rock and heaving it toward Jackie. The rock skittered across the sidewalk, bounced off the step, and landed near Jackie's feet.

Jackie felt anger rising up within him again. "I wasn't bothering that girl," he thought. "She was bothering me."

He thought about his options. He could ignore the man and continue his sweeping. He could shout back at the man. He could run inside and tell his mother what had happened.

The man bent down to pick up another rock.

Jackie stopped wondering what he should do. Furious, he quickly picked up the rock on the sidewalk in front of him. Planting his left foot the way he'd seen baseball players do it, Jackie shifted his weight back on his other foot. Smoothly, he moved his body forward, bringing the rock over his head and whipping it as hard as he could at the man.

The rock hurtled through the air directly at the man's head. The man dove out of the way.

The rock just missed him. Jackie picked up another rock, planted his foot steadily, and hurled it at the man as he was getting up. The rock struck the man on the leg.

Jackie picked up another rock. The man dashed up the steps to his house. Jackie threw the rock just as the man's screen door slammed. The rock clattered off the railing.

"I'm gonna call the cops on you!" the man shouted from behind his door. "You people just don't know how to behave like civilized human beings!"

Jackie's chest was heaving. He was filled with hatred and anger and humiliation. But a tiny part of him also felt *good*. He felt good because he fought back. He didn't just take it. He decided right there that nobody would *ever* treat him like that and get away with it.

Jackie finished his sweeping and went inside his house. He had survived his first experience with racism. It would by no means be his last.

A New Life

"Tell us the story, Mom!" asked Willa Mae Robinson. The Robinson family gathered on the porch of their little house on Pepper Street.

"Oh, not again!" groaned Mrs. Mallie Robinson. "That's ancient history."

"It was just seven years ago, Mom," Mack Robinson pointed out.

"I've told you that story a million times," Mallie complained. "You children need to go to bed. You have school tomorrow."

"*Pleeeeeeeeeeeeaaaaaase?*" five young voices begged.

"Well . . . okay," Mrs. Robinson sighed.

The stars were beginning to come out in the sky as Mallie settled into her rocking chair. Her children crowded around her, elbowing their way so they could be closest to their mother.

The oldest was seventeen-year-old Edgar. On the other side of Mrs. Robinson sat Frank, who was sixteen, and Mack, thirteen. On the floor at Mrs. Robinson's feet sat eleven-year-old Willa Mae and the "baby" of the household, eight-year-old Jackie.

"My grandfather was a slave," Mrs. Robinson began softly.

The Robinson children knew that until the end of the Civil War, black people were brought over from Africa in ships and forced to live and work in America. They couldn't vote. They weren't paid. They didn't have the freedom to go wherever they wanted, or do what they wanted. Many white people treated African-Americans as less than human, almost as if they were animals.

"All five of you were born in a little farmhouse just outside Cairo, Georgia," Mrs. Robinson continued. "It's in Grady County. Southern Georgia. Just above Florida. The soil was red clay, and we grew turnips, cotton, peanuts, corn, and potatoes. We raised hogs, turkeys, and chickens."

"What about our daddy?" Jackie asked.

"Don't be asking about Daddy," Edgar snapped angrily. "Daddy was a bad man."

"Hush, Edgar," Mrs. Robinson said softly. She sighed as she stroked her youngest son's head. "Jackie was too little to know. The boy's got to be told at some point. Your daddy's name was Jerry Robinson. He couldn't read or write, so the best job he could get was working on a plantation for twelve dollars."

"Twelve dollars a *week*?" Mack asked.

"No," Mrs. Robinson replied. "Twelve dollars a *month*. It was one step up from slavery. You see, that's why I always tell you kids how important it is to study hard and do well in school. Anyhow, your daddy didn't like farming. One day he told me that he wanted to move to a city and get a job."

"But you wouldn't go, right, Mom?" asked Willa Mae happily.

"I had your five mouths to feed. At least on the farm I could get enough food for you all. Your daddy and I argued about it. And then one day—I remember it was almost six months to the day after Jackie was born—your daddy told me he was going to visit his brother in Texas."

"Did he?" Jackie asked.

"I don't know," Mallie replied. "I never heard from him again."

There was silence as all five Robinson children thought about what their mother had said. The sound of crickets chirping was all that could be heard.

"Where is our daddy now?" Jackie asked.

"I do not know," Mrs. Robinson said firmly, "and I do not care."

"So you came to California, right, Mom?" Willa Mae asked excitedly.

"Don't be getting ahead of me, Willa Mae. When your daddy left, Mr. Sasser, the owner of the plantation, told me to get off his land."

"So what did you do?" Willa Mae asked.

"It was hard times for me. I was thirty years old. I had five kids. No husband. No job. No money. I looked around and saw nothing but poverty and prejudice. So I decided to go. Somewhere. Anywhere."

"To California, right, Mom?" Willa Mae chirped.

"To California. My brother, your uncle Burton, lived here in Pasadena. He told me to come out here and move in with him until I could get my own place. So I sold all the furniture we had and a lot of our clothes too until I had enough money to buy train tickets. My sister, your aunt Cora, and her family did the same. And I still remember that

night—May 21, 1920—thirteen of us got on the train—"

"The Freedom Train, right, Mom?"

"That's what I called it. It pulled in at midnight. We said our good-byes to our friends and the few relatives who decided to stay in Georgia. I had three dollar bills sewn into the lining of my coat. It was all the money I had in the world. And I carried baby Jackie—he was just sixteen months old—in my arms onto that train. He slept most of the way to California. It was the start of a new life for us."

Mallie put her hands on the wooden armrests of the rocking chair and leaned forward. The children knew story time was over.

"Tell us more, Mom!" Jackie begged. "*Pleeeeeeeeease?*"

"Hush!" Mrs. Robinson said softly. "Now go to bed. All of you."

Doing Good Brings Good

Twelve miles east of Los Angeles, California, is a much smaller city named Pasadena. It is just below the San Gabriel Mountains, which gives the area its warm, dry air. The word *Pasadena* means "the valley" in the language of the Chippewa Indians who settled there hundreds of years ago.

When the Robinson family left Georgia and arrived in Pasadena in 1920, it was like they had entered an entirely new world.

Pasadena was one of the wealthiest cities in the United States. The streets were filled with mansions, and millionaires. The three dollars sewn into the lining of Mallie Robinson's coat would not last long.

The Robinsons squeezed into Uncle Burton's three-room apartment. The first thing Mallie did was get a job to support her family. It wasn't hard to find work as a cleaning lady for the wealthy white people of Pasadena.

Every morning Mallie woke up before daylight and tiptoed out of the apartment so she wouldn't wake up the children. After a long day of housecleaning, clothes washing, and ironing for *other* people, she returned home, exhausted, to her own family. She never complained. Her pay—eight dollars a week.

The Robinson children, with the exception of Jackie, were enrolled in school. Jackie was too young to go to school, and there was no such thing as day care in the 1920s. He couldn't come with Mallie when she went to work, and he was too young to be left home by himself.

"Jackie can come to school with me, Mom," suggested Willa Mae.

Mallie had no other choice, so she brought up the idea with Willa Mae's kindergarten teacher the next time they spoke. The teacher said it would be fine to bring Jackie to school, just as long as he stayed in the playground and didn't disturb the class.

So the next day Willa Mae came to school with her little brother, Jackie, toddling along next to her. She parked Jackie in the sandbox out in the school yard.

"You be good now," she instructed Jackie as she ran inside school.

Every few minutes Willa Mae peeked out the window to see if Jackie was all right. Jackie played in the sandbox all day. When school was dismissed, Willa Mae brushed the sand off him and took him home.

Until Jackie was old enough to be enrolled in the school, he spent most of his days playing in that sandbox. On rainy days Willa Mae's teacher would come out and bring Jackie into the kindergarten room.

With her mother out working in other people's houses a good part of the time, Willa Mae became the lady of the house. As she grew older, she learned how to cook meals and clean up after her four brothers. She went to the store for groceries. Because Jackie was so small, Willa Mae had to take care of him. She would feed him, dress him, and bathe him.

In the middle of the wealth of Pasadena, the Robinsons were very poor. Mallie needed to save every penny she earned. The children didn't receive an allowance. They didn't get presents. The only toys they had were ones other people threw away.

On Saturday nights Mallie would go to the local bakery before it closed to see if they had any leftover bread that hadn't been sold that week. Sometimes the milkman would stop at the end of his route and give her a bottle of leftover milk if it hadn't spoiled.

Often, there wasn't enough food to go around and the Robinsons only ate two meals that day. When Jackie was in kindergarten, he came to school so hungry that his teacher, Miss Gilbert, would bring in sandwiches for him to eat.

After school all the Robinson children worked. They would shine shoes, deliver groceries, or run errands for people. When Jackie was old enough, he had a paper route. He mowed lawns to earn a few pennies. He even sold hot dogs at the Rose Bowl, the famous football stadium nearby.

Eventually, the Robinson family saved enough money so that Mallie could put a down payment on a little house at 121 Pepper Street in Pasadena, which she called "The Castle."

Most kids growing up in nice neighborhoods today take their homes for granted. But to the Robinson kids, The Castle was amazing. It had a backyard and a nice front lawn with flower beds. There was an apple, orange, and peach tree on the property, so if they were hungry they could just reach up and take a piece of fruit. To Mack, Edgar, Frank, Willa Mae, and Jackie, this was amazing.

Mallie Robinson was proud of her new home, and was quick to offer a bed to any visiting relatives who needed a place to stay. Sometimes this would make her children angry.

"Why do you have to be so nice to everybody?" they would complain. "Nobody even says thank you."

"Doing good brings good," she would simply reply.

But if Mallie Robinson thought California was going to be a paradise, she was mistaken. As it turned out, African-Americans were treated no better in Pasadena than they had been in Georgia.

In Pasadena, North Fair Oaks Street was the dividing line between where the black people lived and the white people lived. Blacks were not allowed to live east of Fair Oaks, north of Washington Boulevard, or west of Lincoln Avenue. But Mallie Robinson bought her house from a white man who didn't care about those rules. Her house on Pepper Street was in a white neighborhood.

When the other people on the block found out that a black family had moved into the neighborhood, they weren't happy about it. They circulated a petition to try and force out the Robinsons. When that didn't work, they tried to buy the house back themselves. But Mallie wouldn't sell it.

A lady named Mrs. Carey lived across the street from the Robinsons. She made it very clear that she disliked and feared black people. Whenever one of the Robinson kids would come out to bounce a ball or roller skate on the street, Mrs. Carey ran inside, slammed her door, and called the police. When the children had to walk to the store, Mallie told them to go in the other direction so they would avoid Mrs. Carey.

One day a note appeared under the Robinson door threatening to burn the house down. Mallie suspected that it was Mrs. Carey's doing, but she wasn't sure. It could have been any of the neighbors.

Nobody ever set the house on fire, but one night somebody put up a large cross on the front lawn and ignited it. The Ku Klux Klan, a hate group, often did this to intimidate blacks, Jews, and other people it didn't like. It was a warning—get out!

But Mallie Robinson wouldn't get out no matter what they did to her. She made it clear to her children and her neighbors that she wasn't afraid.

Eventually, the white families on Pepper

Street came to realize they could not intimidate Mallie Robinson. They even came to accept her. They saw Mallie's quiet dignity. They saw how hard she worked to support her family. They saw how much she loved her children and how carefully she raised them. In time, they even came to admire her.

The white families on Pepper Street never became close friends with the Robinsons, but they learned to live on the street together.

That wasn't true of the rest of the city. When Jackie Robinson was a boy in the 1920s, there were no black policemen, firemen, teachers, or janitors in Pasadena. Black people were not allowed to stay in the same hotels, eat in the same restaurants, or play at the same recreational facilities as white people. They could go to the Kress soda fountain, but nobody would wait on them.

When Mallie tried to sign her children up to join the local YMCA, they were refused membership. No reason was given. When the Robinson children were lucky enough to have money to go to the movies, the usher escorted them upstairs to the balcony where all the black people had to sit as a group. Settled into their seats, they hardly ever saw a black person on the screen.

That was what everyday life was like for African-Americans in the 1920s.

One hot summer Sunday afternoon, Mallie took the children to Brookside Park for a picnic. When they finished eating, the kids played hide-and-seek. Jackie ran all over the park looking for hiding places. Finally he came to a big fence with a sign on it that read BROOKSIDE PLUNGE.

He looked through the fence and saw a huge swimming pool. Hundreds of kids were in it, splashing and laughing. Jackie didn't notice that all the children in the pool were white. He stared through the fence for a

BROOKSIDE
PLUNGE

long time as the sun baked down on him.

"There you are!" Mallie said, grabbing him from behind. "We've been looking all over for you."

"Can we go swimming, Mom?" Jackie asked. "Please?"

Mallie Robinson sighed. "Some Tuesday," she said. "I'll take off work early some Tuesday and take you swimming."

"Why not today?" Jackie pleaded. "You're not working today."

"Tuesday is the only day they let colored people into the pool," Mallie said, the bitterness rising in her voice. "Every Tuesday night, they drain the pool and fill it with clean water for the white people on Wednesday."

"Why don't they want colored kids to swim with the white kids, Mom?"

"When you grow up, maybe you'll understand."

"When I grow up, I'm going to swim whenever I *want*," Jackie insisted.

"I hope you will," Mallie said, patting her son on the head. "I hope you will."

* * *

When Jackie was ten years old, the stock market crashed and America tumbled into what was called the Great Depression. Millions of people lost their jobs or their life savings.

White and black families alike were hit by the depression. Even the people on Pepper Street who still hated the Robinsons had things to worry about that were much more important than the presence of a black family in the neighborhood.

One evening there was a knock at the door. Mallie opened it and was startled to see Mrs. Carey standing there. Mrs. Carey had never come over before. In fact, she had never said a kind word to any of the Robinsons. Mallie politely ushered her inside, as the children looked on in amazement.

"I'm sorry to bother you," Mrs. Carey said,

an embarrassed look on her face. "My husband lost his job and . . . can I borrow a cup of milk? It's for the baby."

Mallie got a bottle of milk and handed it to Mrs. Carey without a word.

When Mrs. Carey left, all the Robinson children surrounded Mallie.

"How could you *do* that, Mom?" they asked. "That lady hates us."

"Doing good brings good," Mallie told them again.

The Pepper Street Gang

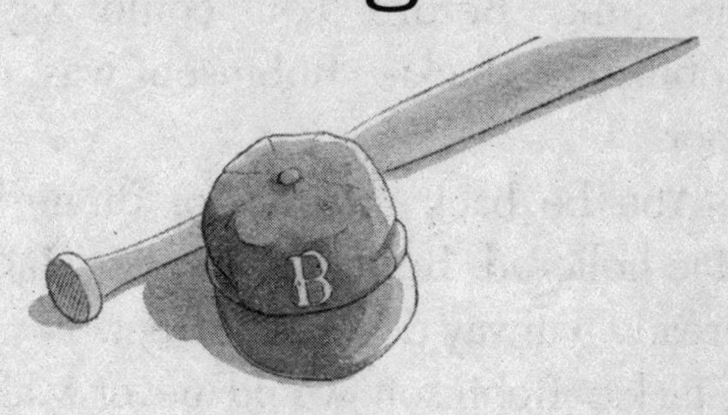

Willa Mae had come home from school and was already starting to prepare dinner when she heard the screen door slam.

"Jackie!" she hollered. "Do you have homework to do?"

Jackie burst into the kitchen like a tornado. In one motion, he slapped his schoolbooks on the table next to the telephone and opened the icebox door. He poured himself a glass of milk and chugged it so fast that some of the milk dribbled down the corners of his mouth.

"Gotta go, Willa Mae!" he said, wiping his mouth with his sleeve as he put the glass in the sink. Before you could say "Jack Robinson," Jackie Robinson was out the door.

"You be back in time for dinner!" Willa Mae hollered. But it was too late. Jackie was already halfway down the street.

Jackie Robinson would never walk when he could run. And he could run like the wind. He figured that the faster he got to the playground, the more time he would have to play before dinnertime. Jackie didn't like being cooped up inside.

"Look at that kid move!" an old white man sitting on a porch said as Jackie zoomed past in a blur.

"Probably stole something," said the lady sitting next to him.

When Jackie arrived at the playground at Washington Elementary School, none of his friends were there yet. But then, running almost as fast as Jackie, Ray Bartlett arrived at the gate.

"Almost beat you this time," Ray huffed. Jackie laughed. Nobody could beat him.

Soon a bunch of other kids showed up at the playground. "Little Jack" Gordon. Woodrow Cunningham and his brother Ernest. George Spivak. Sid Heard and his cousin Van Wade. Walter Dorn. Tim and Bill Herrera. George, Frankie, and Ben Ito. Little Danny Galvin. Shig Kawai.

"What do you want to play?" somebody asked.

"Anything," Jackie replied. "Who's got a ball?"

All the Robinson kids loved sports, including Willa Mae. Jackie learned how to play football, basketball, baseball, soccer, handball, marbles, and badminton from his older brothers. Being the youngest in his family, he was also the smallest. But he made up for his lack of size and strength with an incredible desire to win. He was good enough to play with his brothers, but usually he played with his friends at the playground.

Ray Bartlett was black, like Jackie. Tim and Bill Herrera were Mexican. Danny Galvin was Irish. Shig Kawai and the Ito brothers were Japanese. Walter Dorn and the Cunningham boys were white.

Some of their parents may have disliked one another, but the boys didn't care what color somebody's skin was or what country they came from. All they cared about was who could put the ball in the hoop. Who could run back a kickoff to put his team in good field position. Who could whack a tennis ball over the fence with a broom handle.

The boys came from all different races, religions, and nationalities. But Jackie and his friends had two things in common. They all loved sports, and they were all very poor. They called themselves the "Pepper Street Gang."

"Let's play dodgeball!" Danny Galvin suggested, bouncing a kickball.

"Yeah!"

The fourteen kids formed a big circle, with each boy about ten feet away from the boy on either side of him. It was Danny's ball, so he got the first shot. He heaved it at Sid, who dashed out of the way. But the ball ticked off Sid's foot.

"You're out!" Danny yelled.

Sid sat down by the fence and the circle closed in a little to fill in his space. Van threw the ball at Frankie, but missed. Ben whipped it at Ernest and plunked him on his rear end. Ray threw it at Tim, but Tim caught it on a fly, so Ray was out. The circle got smaller.

"Throw it at me!" Jackie yelled.

"No way!" said Woodrow. "You're too quick. Nobody can hit you."

One by one, the boys were knocked out of the game and the circle closed in tighter. Finally, the only boys left were Shig,

Woodrow, and Jackie. They formed a triangle.

"Get 'em, Shig!" somebody yelled.

"C'mon, Jackie!"

Shig looked menacingly at Jackie and prepared to throw. But at the last instant, he whirled around and whipped the ball toward Woodrow, who was taken by surprise, and couldn't get out of the way in time. The ball glanced off his shoulder.

"You're out!" Shig yelled.

Now it was down to Jackie and Shig. Jackie picked up the ball and stared at Shig.

"You're dead meat," he said good-naturedly.

"You wish," Shig replied.

Shig darted left, then right trying to fake out Jackie. Jackie pretended he was going to throw the ball at Shig's feet, then at his head. At the side, the Pepper Street Gang cheered enthusiastically. Finally, after a minute of this cat-and-mouse game, Jackie wound up and threw.

The ball flew directly at Shig's face. He had

fast reflexes, and he ducked. But not quickly enough. The ball bonked him on the forehead as he fell backward out of the way.

"I win!" Jackie yelled, raising his arms in triumph.

The ball, however, bounced off Shig's head and flew directly up in the air. It looked like he had done a "header" in soccer. As Shig tumbled to the ground, he saw the ball rising above him. If he could grab it on the fly, he knew, Jackie would be out.

As he hit the blacktop, Shig reached his arms out. The ball came down and somehow landed in Shig's hands. He hugged it to his chest.

"You're out!" Shig yelled. "I win!"

All the other boys cheered Shig's great play. Stunned, Jackie fell to his knees. "That's not fair!" he complained. "I hit him! He was out. It was a lucky bounce!"

And then he began to cry.

The boys were embarrassed. They all cried

now and then, but nobody wanted to do it in front of his friends. Most of the boys walked off to the side to give Jackie some privacy. They knew how competitive he was. But Shig got up off the blacktop and went over to him.

"It's no big deal," Shig told Jackie. "It's just a game. You win almost every game we play."

"I don't like to lose," Jackie sniffed. "*Ever.*"

After a few minutes Jackie got control of himself. He congratulated Shig on his great play and they joined the rest of the boys, who had started a spirited game of punchball.

But the whole time during the punchball game, Jackie kept thinking about the dodgeball game. *What could I have done to win?* he asked himself. The next time, he decided, he would aim for Shig's feet instead of his head. That way, it would be nearly impossible for Shig to catch the ball.

After the punchball game was over, Frankie spotted a tennis ball stuck in a sewer grating. Almost instantly, the Pepper Street

Gang was involved in a rousing handball game against the wall of the school. It was starting to get dark outside, but nobody seemed to notice.

That's when Jackie's sister, Willa Mae, appeared at the gate of the playground.

"Jackie Robinson!" she hollered.

"Uh-oh," Jackie moaned.

"You come home right now!" Willa Mae insisted. "I *told* you to be back in time for dinner."

The rest of the Pepper Street Gang giggled as Jackie was led away by his big sister.

All the Kids I Beat

All the boys in the Pepper Street Gang were good athletes, but Jackie was the best. He seemed to have a natural ability to pick up just about any sport and excel at it right away. Sometimes, during gym class at school, other kids would offer him part of their lunch if he would play on their team. They knew that with Jackie on a team, there was a good chance that team would win.

One summer day some of the guys in the Pepper Street Gang were hanging around Brookside Park. A bunch of people had gathered over by the rec center, so the boys went to see what was happening.

PASADENA PING-PONG CHAMPIONSHIPS, read the banner on the wall. In smaller letters, it said the tournament was open to all boys and girls. The grand prize was ten dollars. There were about a dozen Ping-Pong tables set up, and kids were furiously slapping the little white balls back and forth at each table.

"I could sure use ten dollars," Ray Bartlett said.

"Me too," Jackie agreed. To most of the kids in the Pepper Street Gang, ten dollars sounded like a million.

"Why don't you enter, Jackie?" Bill Herrera suggested.

"I don't know how to play Ping-Pong," Jackie replied.

"So what?" Bill said, pointing at a boy who had just missed the ball. "It doesn't look hard. All you have to do is hit that dinky ball over the net so it lands on the other side of the table."

"I don't know . . . " Jackie said dubiously.

"Yeah, you're probably right, Jackie," Ray said as he winked at Bill. "There's no way *you* could beat any of *these* kids. They look pretty good. Much better than you."

"I'll enter," Jackie said firmly. He could never resist a challenge.

Jackie filled out the entry form and was paired with a tall, skinny boy who looked about thirteen years old. They were each handed a paddle and assigned to a table. The tall kid took a ball from a box. The Pepper Street Gang gathered at the side to offer Jackie advice and encouragement.

"Volley for serve," the tall kid said.

"Okay," said Jackie, who had no idea what that meant.

The tall kid hit the ball softly over the net so it bounced on Jackie's side. Jackie tapped it back carefully with his paddle. The tall kid hit it softly again, and Jackie returned it. A third time the tall kid lobbed the ball to

Jackie's side of the table, and Jackie tapped it back.

"Hey look, you guys," Jackie yelled to his friends. "I'm pretty good at this!"

The next time the ball got to the tall kid, he didn't lob it back at Jackie. He brought back his paddle and slammed the ball. It skipped off Jackie's side of the table and past him before he had the chance to put his paddle up.

"Hey!" Jackie exclaimed. "No fair!"

"You've got to keep it low," one of Jackie's friends advised. "Don't let him whack it."

"*Now* you tell me," Jackie complained.

"I serve first," the tall kid said. "I'll go easy on you."

Jackie's eyes flashed anger. He didn't need anybody to go easy on him. "Just play your best," he told the kid.

The tall kid served low and hard and the ball skipped past Jackie. He realized he would have to react more quickly. He got his paddle on the next serve, but hit the ball too far and it sailed over the table. He hit the next serve back on the table, but again the tall kid won the point. The score reached 5–0.

Jackie walked over to his friends for a pep talk.

"Use your backhand!" Ray whispered.

"I have a left hand and a right hand," Jackie replied. "What's a backhand?"

Jackie returned to the table and served. The tall kid hit it back and Jackie hit it back again. He was getting the feel of the game. He was beginning to figure out how hard he could hit the ball without hitting it off the table. He learned the angle he had to hold the paddle to send the ball just above the net. His natural quickness and reflexes made it possible for him to reach just about any shot. He won his first point on a hard, crosscourt winner that the tall kid couldn't reach.

It occurred to Jackie that if he hit the ball all the way to one corner of the table and then hit the next shot all the way to the *other* corner, he could get his opponent running back and forth. The strategy worked, and he started winning more points than he was losing. Before long, the score was 14–13 in favor of Jackie.

"Thanks for going easy on me," Jackie said to the tall kid.

"Shut up and serve."

Jackie served and the tall kid's return sailed wide of the table. He smacked his paddle against the table in frustration. Jackie won the next three points too. The tall kid was flustered now and couldn't seem to do anything right. When the score reached 21–16, he stormed away from the table in disgust.

"Where's he going?" Jackie asked. "I was just getting warmed up."

"Twenty-one points wins the game, Jackie!" Ray hollered. "You *beat* that kid!"

Jackie was embarrassed for not knowing how many points he needed to win. But that didn't stop him from trouncing his next opponent, a girl who brought her own orange paddle from home. He beat her 21–3. With each point, Jackie became more confident and better at the game.

After defeating three other kids, Jackie advanced to the quarterfinals, then the semifinals, and finally . . . the finals.

One of the tables was carried to the middle of the basketball court. All the kids jockeyed for position around it to get the best view of the final game.

The other finalist was a boy named Angel. Jackie had seen a little of Angel's last game, and he was worried. Instead of gripping the paddle by the handle like most everyone else, Angel wrapped his hand around the fat part of the paddle. He hit the ball in a way that put a vicious spin on it and sent it off on some crazy bounces when it got to the other side of the table. To make things even more confusing, Angel was a left-hander.

Jackie and Angel were introduced to the crowd, and everyone cheered enthusiastically.

"You can beat him, Jackie," the Pepper Street Gang shouted.

The two boys volleyed for serve and Angel won. His serve was difficult to read, but after seeing it a few times, Jackie got the hang of which direction the ball was going to bounce. He was behind by the score of 3–2 when it was his turn to serve.

Angel won some points with his tricky spins, and Jackie won some thanks to his quickness and agility. The two were pretty evenly matched, and the score was tight. It was all tied up at 19–19, and it was Angel's serve. The Pepper Street Gang informed Jackie that in Ping-Pong, a player has to be ahead by two points to win the game.

Angel flicked the serve to Jackie's left. Jackie, who still didn't know what a backhand was, backhanded it across the net. Angel tried to flick it down the right side, but the ball skimmed an inch over the table. Jackie had the lead, 20–19. One more point and the championship would be his.

Angel served again, and Jackie had no trouble making the return. Angel kept trying to throw Jackie off balance with his spins, but each time Jackie could tell which way the ball was going to bounce by watching Angel's paddle as it hit the ball. Angel was playing carefully, knowing that if he made one mistake the game was all over.

The ball was whizzing back and forth over and over again. Jackie and Angel were focusing all their attention on the ball.

At last, Jackie saw an opening. His last shot had forced Angel all the way to the right side of the table. Angel's return shot was right down the middle. It was easy for Jackie to handle. With a flick of his wrist, Jackie zipped the ball across the left side of the table. Angel dove for it, but the ball ticked off the end of his paddle.

"Yes!" Jackie screamed, throwing his arms in the air. The Pepper Street Gang went wild. As Jackie and Angel shook hands, the announcement came over the loudspeaker that Jackie was the Ping-Pong champion of Pasadena.

A local politician came forward and handed Jackie a certificate and a ten-dollar bill.

"You're pretty good, son," he told Jackie as a photographer snapped their picture. "How long have you been playing?"

"About an hour and a half," Jackie replied.

The Pepper Street Gang gathered around Jackie to look at the ten-dollar bill like it was a precious jewel.

"What are you going to do with it?" Ray asked Jackie.

"I've got a plan," he said.

Jackie ran all the way home, holding the ten-dollar bill tightly in his fist. His mother was on the porch when he arrived, sitting in her rocking chair.

Award

"Hey, Mom," Jackie yelled, all out of breath. "I've got a surprise for you!"

"I've seen everything," Mallie Robinson replied. "Nothing could surprise me."

"Close your eyes and hold out your hand."

Mallie did as Jackie instructed. He placed the ten-dollar bill in her hand and told her to open her eyes.

"My Lord!" Mallie Robinson exclaimed. She had to work all week to earn ten dollars.

"It's for you, Mom!" Jackie told her. "I know how hard you work to take care of us all, and I wanted to give you something back."

"You didn't steal it, I hope."

"No, Mom, I *won* it."

"Won it?" Mallie asked. "Doing what?"

"Playing Ping-Pong, Mom! I'm the Ping-Pong champ of Pasadena!"

"Ping-Pong?" Mallie knew perfectly well that Jackie had never played Ping-Pong in his life. "Who taught you how to play Ping-Pong?"

"All the kids I beat."

Trouble on Pepper Street

"What do you want to do?" Ray Bartlett asked Jackie one summer day.

"Play ball," Jackie replied. "You want to play ball?"

"It's too hot," Ray said. "Must be a hundred and fifty degrees out."

"I wish we could go for a swim," Jackie mused.

It may not have been a hundred and fifty degrees, but it was very hot. Brookside

Plunge was closed to African-Americans, and there was no other public pool open to them.

"Hey, I know where we can swim," Ray said, brightening.

"Where?"

"The reservoir."

"Swimming's not allowed in the reservoir," Jackie pointed out. "Not even for whites."

"So what? We won't get caught. Besides, if I don't get into water soon, I'm gonna melt."

Ray and Jackie hiked several miles to the reservoir. By the time they got there, sweat was dripping off them. There was a ten-foot chain fence around the reservoir, and a big sign that said, NO TRESPASSING. VIOLATORS WILL BE PUNISHED TO THE FULL EXTENT OF THE LAW.

"Let's go home, Ray," Jackie suggested. "I don't like this."

"C'mon," Ray urged. "We came all the way out here. Nobody's around. I'm sweating like a pig."

The two boys climbed to the top of the fence and hopped over it. Ray didn't hesitate a moment. He stripped off all his clothes and dove in the water. Jackie looked around nervously.

"It feels great, Jackie!" Ray shouted gleefully when his head popped up to the surface. "What are you, chicken?"

Reluctantly, Jackie took off his clothes and waded into the water. Ray was right. It *did* feel great. As soon as his body was under the water, the heat of the day seemed to vanish.

As Jackie swam around, he stopped worrying about getting caught and began to enjoy himself. He and Ray had a splashing contest. They competed to see who could stay underwater the longest.

They were having so much fun, they didn't notice that a police car had pulled up.

"Hey, you kids!" shouted Captain Hugh Morgan, the head of the Pasadena police youth division. "Get out of there! Now!"

When Jackie and Ray realized what was happening, they looked at each other in panic. They couldn't run. They didn't even have on bathing suits. Embarrassed and ashamed, they got out of the water and quickly pulled their pants on.

"Get in the car," was all Captain Morgan said.

Ray and Jackie climbed in the back of the patrol car silently. Jackie was nervous. Where were they being taken? To jail? Would this be on his record for the rest of his life? He glanced at Ray, who looked just as frightened.

Captain Morgan pulled up to the police station and escorted the boys inside. He made them sit on a cold bench in a bare room for a long time. Finally, Jackie's mother arrived. She spoke with Captain Morgan for a few minutes, signed some papers, and took both boys home. Mallie didn't have to hit Jackie or yell at him. All she had to do was give him a long, hard stare. Jackie felt angry, embarrassed, and humiliated.

* * *

Jackie, Ray, and the rest of the Pepper Street Gang were not angels. They loved sports, but sometimes they also liked getting into mischief. They would steal food from a neighborhood fruit stand. They would throw dirt bombs at cars.

A new golf course had recently been opened in Pasadena. The Pepper Street Gang found a way to make money at the golf course. They didn't get jobs as caddies. They would hide in the trees at the edge of the fairways. When a golfer hit a ball into the woods, the boys would sneak out from behind the trees, grab the ball, and run away with it. Then they would wash all the balls. At the end of the day they would go to the parking lot and sell the balls to golfers as they were getting into their cars.

In time, the Pepper Street Gang found

themselves spending less time playing sports and more time getting into trouble. Jackie was never a great student at school, but in fifth grade his report card began to slip from B's and C's to C's and D's. After school, he had to spend more and more time with Police Captain Morgan.

One day Jackie was walking down Pepper Street, heading for the playground to meet the gang. As he turned the corner onto Morton Street, a man called him over.

"C'mere," the man said.

"Me?"

"Yeah, you."

The man's name was Carl Anderson. He was a black man in his early twenties. Anderson worked as a mechanic at the garage on the corner of Mountain and Morton Streets. Jackie had seen him many times before, but the two had never spoken. Jackie thought about making a run for it, but Mr. Anderson didn't look threatening, so Jackie went over to him.

"What do you want, mister?" Jackie asked.

"I've been watching you and your friends," Mr. Anderson said softly. "And I don't like what I see."

"Oh yeah?" Jackie got defensive. Typical adult, telling kids how they should run their lives.

"Stealing. Pulling pranks. Getting in trouble with the police. Is that how you want to live your life?"

Jackie looked at his shoes. "I should have made a run for it," he thought to himself. "Then I wouldn't have to be listening to this."

"I used to be like you," Mr. Anderson continued. "And then somebody pulled me aside and told me something that changed my life."

"Yeah, what?" Jackie was curious, if nothing else.

"He told me that if I kept doing what I was doing, I would not only be hurting myself, but I would be hurting my mother too."

Jackie looked up from his shoes.

"That's right. My mother worked day and night to raise me and my sisters. One day I got caught stealing candy from a store and my mother had to come to the police station to bring me home. I saw the look in her eyes. Her disappointment in me. I had let her down. And from that moment on, I resolved that I would never get into any trouble again. And I never have. I did that for my mother, and I did it for me too."

Jackie thought about the day he was caught swimming in the reservoir and his mother had to come get him. He remembered the same look in her eyes.

"You're a good kid," Mr. Anderson told Jackie. "I can see that. You just go along with the crowd because you're afraid those boys will think you're different. You're afraid they'll think you're afraid to do something. Well, it doesn't take any guts to follow a crowd. It takes guts to be willing to be different. Someday you'll admit I'm right."

Jackie scuffed his shoe against the pavement. He wasn't going to admit it, but Jackie already knew Mr. Anderson was right. Jackie loved his mother more than anyone else in the whole world. He decided right then that he would never do anything that might get him into trouble again.

A Rising Star

As Jackie and his friends became teenagers, the Pepper Street Gang began to go its separate ways. Some of the boys got jobs, which left little time for hanging around the street. Others became interested in cars or girls.

Jackie Robinson's passion was sports. He was up to 135 pounds when he turned sixteen and became a freshman at John Muir Technical High School in Pasadena. He was strong and lean.

After gym class at one of the first days of

school, the gym teacher walked over to Jackie and pulled him aside.

"You look like you might be a good athlete," the teacher said. "Have you ever played sports?"

"A little," Jackie said modestly.

"I coach the football team. Why don't you come out to the practice field after school today?"

"Okay."

Jackie had played touch football with the Pepper Street Gang in the playground, but he had never played any sport in an organized league. He liked the idea. In high school there would be real uniforms, and good equipment. He'd play on a real field, not a blacktop. There would be coaches, referees, and cheering fans.

After school Jackie went to the practice field. The football team was already there, doing stretching exercises. The coach gave Jackie a pair of shoulder pads. There was no extra pair of cleats, so Jackie had to play in his sneakers.

"I like the way you ran in gym class," the coach said. "Can you run with a football?"

"A little."

The coach lined up the offense and defense and whispered to the quarterback that he should take the snap and hand the football off to Jackie to see what he could do with it.

"Hut-one . . . hut-two . . . hike!"

The center hiked the ball to the quarterback. He took two steps back, spun, and stuck the football in Jackie's stomach. Jackie wrapped both hands around the ball and looked for running room in front of him.

There wasn't any. Just a tangled mess of offensive and defensive players pushing against one another and grunting. Jackie saw that he couldn't run forward. He cut left so he could sneak around the linemen. One of the defensive ends saw Jackie coming and dove at him. Jackie threw him a hip fake and the kid went flying by.

Jackie dug in his sneaker and cut right. Now he was into the secondary. Several defensive players converged on him. Jackie faked out one, then another. He scampered down the left sideline, with five players in pursuit.

They didn't have a chance. Jackie was pulling away when he crossed the goal line.

When the coach caught up with Jackie, his eyes were lit up with excitement. He kept bubbling about how he had never seen a boy run so fast. The coach marveled at how Jackie was able to stop and suddenly change directions even though he was wearing sneakers.

"Can you throw the ball?" he asked Jackie.

"A little."

The coach brought Jackie out to the middle of the field and instructed another player to set up at the ten-yard line to catch the ball.

"See how far you can heave it, son," the coach told Jackie.

Jackie placed his fingertips on the seams and wrapped his hand around the football. He took a few steps behind the fifty-yard line and ran up to the line. As his foot touched it, he let the ball fly.

The player who had been assigned to catch the football at the ten-yard line didn't even move. The ball sailed far over his head, over the goal line, and through the goal posts. It traveled at least sixty yards in the air. A perfect spiral.

"That freshman kid threw a field goal from the fifty-yard line!" exclaimed one of the players.

The regular starting quarterback looked on with awe, and then envy. He couldn't throw a football nearly that far. He knew that from that moment on, he would be the *backup* quarterback.

* * *

Jackie made the football team, of course. He led the Muir Terriers to a winning season.

When football season was over and basketball season began, the coach of the basketball team came over to Jackie.

"Can you shoot?" he asked.

"A little."

After seeing Jackie shoot, dribble, pass, and rebound, the coach immediately put him in the starting lineup. Playing guard, Jackie quickly became a team leader.

When basketball season ended and tryouts for the track team were held, it was no surprise to anyone when Jackie showed up. He had already demonstrated in football and basketball how fast he could run. For the Muir track team, he competed in the long jump, pole vault, and high jump.

Track season was already underway when a sign-up sheet was posted in the gym for baseball tryouts. Jackie wasn't sure he was going to try out for baseball. Of all the sports he played, he was weakest at baseball. Besides, baseball and track were held during the same season. It would be difficult to compete at both sports and also get his schoolwork done. Plus, Jackie sang in the school glee club.

"I don't see your name on my sign-up sheet," the baseball coach said to Jackie one day.

"I'm not that good at baseball," Jackie replied.

"Yeah," the coach sighed. "You're right. All these other guys are probably a lot better than you are."

Jackie grabbed a pen and put his name on the sign-up sheet. Nobody was going to tell *him* he wasn't good enough. He became one of the best players on the team, playing shortstop and catcher.

When school let out for the summer, Jackie was bored hanging around Pepper Street. He happened to see a sign announcing the Pacific Coast Negro Tennis Tournament. Jackie had never played tennis before. But it didn't look that different from Ping-Pong, and he had mastered that game in an afternoon. Jackie entered the tennis tournament. Even though he had never played tennis before, he picked up the game immediately and shocked everyone by winning the tournament.

Everybody has a special skill. Some people are good at cooking. Others are good with numbers. Still others have a knack for being able to fix things that are broken. Jackie Robinson was good at every sport he tried. He was a great all-around athlete, and he began to receive acclaim for his skill.

Sports, he realized, could be more than a way to have fun and burn off extra energy. He liked the sound of hundreds of people cheering when he ran for a touchdown, sank a basket, or hit a home run. Those people in the stands cheer or boo because of what a player does on the field, he noticed, not because the player happens to have dark or light skin.

This had a big impact on Jackie. He was starting to think about what he wanted to be when he grew up. He decided that one way or another, sports would be his life.

There was a small problem, though. African-Americans were not allowed to play professional sports. There hadn't been a black player in major league baseball since they were banned from the game in the 1880s. The National Football League also barred blacks from playing. The National Basketball Association hadn't even been formed yet, and there was no such thing as professional track and field either.

Becoming a professional athlete was not a career choice for a young black athlete in the 1930s. All Jackie Robinson could hope for was to get a job as a coach. So that's what he aimed for.

In the meantime he was swiftly becoming recognized as one of the best young athletes in the United States.

The funny thing was, Jackie was only the *second* best athlete in the Robinson family.

The World Stage

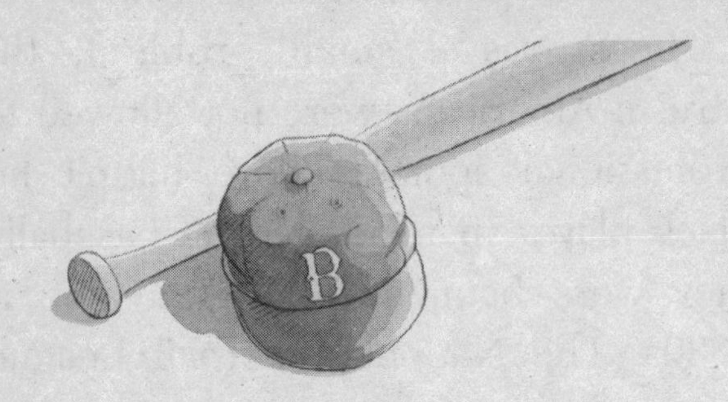

The Robinson family gathered in their living room on Pepper Street. They huddled around a radio that was about the size of today's television sets. It was 1936, and Mallie Robinson's children weren't kids anymore. Edgar was twenty-six years old. Jackie, the "baby" of the family, was seventeen.

"Quiet, everybody!" Jackie said as he turned the radio dial carefully. "I'm trying to tune it in."

Jackie was straining to find the right station through the music, voices, and static that

jumbled up the airwaves. Suddenly, out of the noise, a man's voice said, "It's cold and it looks like rain in Berlin today. But our American boys are hoping to put on a show and bring home some gold, silver, and bronze medals to show Hitler just who is the best in the world . . . "

"That's it!" Mallie shouted. "Hush, everyone!"

There was no television in 1936. No Internet. The only way to experience the Summer Olympics as it was happening was to listen to the radio, or to *be* in Berlin, Germany.

Mallie, Jackie, Edgar, Frank, and Willa Mae Robinson were listening to the radio. Mack Robinson was in Berlin, a member of the United States track team.

While Jackie always played just about every sport he could find, Mack focused all his concentration on track. At twenty-two he was one of the fastest sprinters in the world.

That was quite a shock to Mallie Robinson. She remembered the day she took ten-year-old Mack to the doctor. When the stethoscope was placed on Mack's chest, the doctor made a face that said he didn't like the sound he was hearing. Mallie was informed that Mack had a bad heart. The doctor said playing sports could be fatal to him.

She tried to stop Mack from competing, but it was impossible. All the Robinson children loved sports. Mack was always able to run faster than everyone else. At Pasadena Junior College, he tried out for the track team and set the junior college long-jump record. After two years he transferred to the University of Oregon where he set the world record in the 220-yard dash.

Jackie idolized Mack. He was so proud that his big brother was competing in the Olympics. He felt a little jealous too. Jackie was becoming a star in Pasadena, but now Mack would be famous all over the world. As he listened intently to the radio, though, Jackie was rooting for Mack all the way.

Everyone in the United States was rooting particularly hard for the American athletes. World War II had not yet begun, but many people could tell it was coming. German dictator Adolf Hitler had made no secret of his plans for worldwide domination.

Hitler had built a huge Olympic stadium that could hold over 100,000 spectators. He was using the Olympic Games as a showcase to the world for Germany and his Nazi Party.

According to Hitler, the German people were superior to all other races and nationalities. He considered black people to be inferior. He especially despised Jewish people.

The American track team was made up of blacks—Mack, Jesse Owens, and Ralph Metcalfe—and Jews—Martin Glickman and Sam Stoller. Jesse Owens, like Mack Robinson, grew up poor. He was the youngest of ten children and the son of a sharecropper in Alabama. But he made it all the way to Ohio State University.

Many Americans felt the United States should have boycotted the Olympics as a protest against Hitler's bigotry. But bigotry was far from absent in America. The decision was made to go ahead and compete against Germany in Berlin.

"Shhhh, everybody!" Jackie said, "they're about to start the 200-meter dash."

"The Olympic record is 21.2 seconds, held by Eddie Tolan," the announcer said. "But Americans Jesse Owens and Mack Robinson hope to shatter that mark."

"That's my boy!" beamed Mallie, tears in her eyes.

"They're on their mark . . . set . . . "

A gunshot was heard.

"It's Owens off to a quick start," the announcer hollered. "Owens and Robinson! Osendarp of Holland right behind them!"

The Robinson family was jumping up and down.

"Owens and Robinson and Osendarp pulling away at the 100-meter mark! The rest of the field is falling back! Owens with Robinson three meters back. Owens wins the gold! Robinson the silver! Americans one and two! Both of them broke the Olympic record! Osendarp is third!"

All across America, and especially on Pepper Street in Pasadena, everyone was going crazy and yelling their heads off. Tears of joy ran down Mallie's cheeks as each of her children hugged her.

Jesse Owens, however, was the hero of the Olympics. He won four gold medals, for the 100 meters, 200 meters, long jump, and 400-meter relay. He set three Olympic records and tied another.

The two Jewish-American athletes, Martin Glickman and Sam Stoller, did not compete. It was felt that their presence on the field would offend the host of the games, Adolf Hitler.

Hitler congratulated all the athletes who won gold medals. But when Jesse Owens and Mack Robinson mounted the victory platform, Hitler left the stadium so he wouldn't have to shake their hands.

That night, Jackie Robinson was so excited, he had trouble sleeping. His big brother had competed and won a medal at the Olympic Games. Mack was one of the fastest men in the world. In twenty seconds, he and Jesse Owens had made a mockery of Hitler's bigoted racial theories. They chased Hitler right out of his own stadium!

Jackie dreamed that someday he too might use his athletic ability to accomplish something so wonderful and powerful. And someday, he would.

A Great Day

"Are you Mack Robinson's little brother?" everybody asked Jackie on the first day of school in September 1937.

"Yes," Jackie replied, both proud and embarrassed. "I am."

It had been Mallie Robinson's dream for her children to go to college. Jackie, like Mack before him, enrolled in Pasadena Junior College (today known as Pasadena City College). PJC was a two-year school. Mallie Robinson could send her children there because tuition was free and the kids could live at home while they attended school.

Because Mack had been to the Olympics and came home a champion, he was a legend on the PJC campus. Jackie loved his brother, but it was a little unsettling. People would always ask him about Mack. People compared him to Mack. Jackie had to follow in his brother's footsteps—footsteps that were two of the fastest in the world.

But Jackie Robinson was a pretty good athlete himself. A few months short of his eighteenth birthday, he had reached his full adult height—five feet eleven inches. He weighed 175 pounds. He wasn't quite as fast a runner as Mack was, but he was more muscular.

Pasadena Junior College was an almost all-white school. Only sixty out of the four thousand students were African-American. Jackie was one of the few black athletes at the school. But he played four sports for the "Bulldogs" and earned varsity letters in all of them.

Football was Jackie's strongest sport. When he wasn't throwing and rushing for touchdowns as the team's quarterback, he was a great blocker. And when the offense wasn't on the field, Jackie played defense and was known for his hard tackling.

The fans called him "Jitterbug Jackie Robinson," after a wild dance craze of the day. Jackie was famous for being able to run at top speed, then stop on a dime, change direction, and dash off at top speed in another direction. Opposing players were left with armfuls of nothing when they tried to tackle Jackie.

Even though he broke an ankle during a practice session in his freshman season, Jackie still made the Junior College All-America team. The next year, the Bulldogs won all eleven of their games and won the Junior College Championship. Jackie scored 131 points and carried the ball for more than one thousand yards.

In baseball, Jackie led off and played shortstop for the Bulldogs. He hit .417 in 1938, striking out only three times all season and stealing twenty-five bases in twenty-four games. He was chosen Most Valuable Player of Southern California junior colleges.

In basketball, Jackie was the leading scorer of his team and in the conference both of his years at PJC.

In track, he ran 100 meters, 200 meters, and competed in the long jump. At first, his efforts didn't compare with Mack's, but Jackie got better and better the more he competed.

Around Pasadena, people *still* talk about what happened on May 7, 1938.

Jackie woke up that Saturday a little nervous, but excited. It was the day of the Southern California Junior College Track Championships. He would be competing in the long jump. He knew all eyes would be on him, because his brother held the national junior college record in that event. He had to wait a long time before it was his turn, which only made him more nervous.

"Just take it easy," his coach told Jackie as he stood at the beginning of the runway. "The idea is to win the competition, not to beat your brother. Do the best you can and don't put too much pressure on yourself."

Jackie placed his toe behind the line and crouched down. He took a deep breath. And then he took off.

In the long jump, the athlete sprints down a runway and then leaps as high and as far as possible, being careful to start the jump behind the line. The landing is in a pit covered with sand. It's very important to land feet first, and then let your body fall forward past the point where your feet hit the sand. As soon as the jumper lands, judges dash over and carefully measure the length of the jump.

Jackie did all that right, except for one thing. In an effort to jump as far as possible, he started the jump just a bit too far forward. His right foot was touching the line when he took off.

"Foul!" called one of the judges.

It was okay. Each jumper gets three chances. Jackie walked back down the runway to try again.

On his second jump, Jackie was very careful not to foul, starting his jump almost a foot behind the takeoff line. He may have been a little too careful. Even though he strained to jump as far as he could, he knew he hadn't gone far enough to win the meet, much less break Mack's record.

"Twenty-three feet, nine inches," called the judge.

That put Jackie in second place. He walked slowly back to the beginning of the runway. He had one more chance. He would need to jump a foot longer to win the meet.

To break Mack's record, he would need to jump almost two feet longer.

Jackie toed the line. He closed his eyes for a few moments to compose himself. And then he took off down the runway.

Arms pumping. Feet pounding. Jackie sprinted down the runway. He spotted the take off point when he was twenty feet away from it. Making some crazy instant calculation in his head, he figured out which foot he would be using for his takeoff. He hit the line and pushed off the ground with as much power as he could generate.

In the air now, Jackie windmilled his arms and legs in a desperate battle against the force of gravity. Gravity always wins, of course. It started pulling Jackie down. He slid his feet out in front of him. He stretched his arms forward, trying to get just a couple of more inches out of the jump.

Finally, he landed in the pit and fell forward. Right away, Jackie felt like he had made his best jump ever.

The judges dashed over with their tape measures. They got down on their hands and knees so they could place the tape at the exact spot where Jackie's heels hit the sand.

"Twenty-five feet, six and one-half inches," hollered a judge.

That did it! Jackie had won the meet easily.

Better still, he broke Mack's record. Jackie now owned the national junior college record for the long jump. The rest of the team gathered around him to offer their congratulations. The crowd went crazy.

But Jackie Robinson's day wasn't over. As it turned out, the Southern California Junior College Baseball Championships were scheduled the same day as the track championship. The track meet was in the morning, and the baseball game in the afternoon.

Jackie could have picked just one of the

sports to compete in. But he was very competitive, and he wanted very badly to participate in both. Also, he didn't want to disappoint his pals on the track team or the baseball team.

"Congratulations," his friend Ray Bartlett yelled after Jackie was awarded his first-place ribbon. "Quick, get in the car!"

Jackie was barely in the passenger seat when Ray peeled out of the parking lot.

Ray was in such a hurry because he had to drive Jackie from Pomona to Glendale, California, where the baseball game was taking place. Back in those days, it was a two-hour drive. That is, as long as the traffic didn't get too heavy or Ray's old car didn't break down.

While Ray drove, Jackie peeled off his tracksuit and pulled on his baseball uniform. Ray had purchased a sandwich in advance, and Jackie ate his lunch in the car. He knew he would miss the beginning of the game, but hoped he could get there early enough to help the team.

Ray found the baseball field and screeched to a stop. Jackie dashed out of the car and found the Pasadena dugout.

"Finally, you're here!" his coach shouted with relief. "Did you win the long jump?"

"Yeah," Jackie replied. "What inning is it?"

"The third," coach told him.

"What's the score?"

"We're losing 3–2," said the coach, handing Jackie a bat. "And you're up."

Jackie approached the plate slowly. He was trying to get his bearings. He didn't even know if he would be facing a lefty or a right-hander. He peeked at the mound and saw the pitcher was a lefty. "Good," he thought. Jackie liked hitting against lefties.

There was a runner on second, Jackie noticed. A single would drive him in and tie the game. Jackie tried to switch his brain over to baseball. Being able to jump twenty-six feet wouldn't help him now. He would have to hit a ball speeding toward him at eighty to ninety miles per hour.

"Let's go, Jackie!" somebody shouted from the bench.

"No batter, no batter," chanted the infielders.

Jackie decided to let the first two pitches go by so he could get a good look at them. The pitcher threw one over the plate for a strike and the other off the outside corner. The count was one ball and one strike.

"Drive me in, Jackie," hollered the runner at second.

Jackie wrapped his hands around the bat handle. If the next pitch was good, he decided, he would take a cut at it. If it was on the corner, he would let it go by. With just one strike on him, there was no point in swinging at a pitch he couldn't hit hard.

The pitcher went into his windup and delivered. Almost immediately, Jackie could tell it was a curveball. He could see the pitcher twist his wrist as he let go of the ball. He could see the seams on the baseball spinning as it sped toward the plate.

Many hitters have a tough time hitting a pitch that curves, but Jackie liked them. Curveballs traveled more slowly than fastballs. That gave him more time to react and adjust his swing.

The ball started out heading for the corner, but Jackie could tell it was going to curve over the plate. His eyes grew wide as he brought the bat around to meet the ball.

Jackie was a little overanxious, so the bat head got to the plate a fraction of a second before the ball did. But he hit it squarely, sending a screaming liner down the third baseline.

The third baseman made a dive to his right, but the ball was already past him when he hit the dirt. The ball skimmed the foul line, kicking up a little puff of chalk dust.

"Fair ball!" the umpire hollered.

Jackie sprinted out of the batter's box, much the same way he sprinted down the runway earlier in the day. The runner on second had taken off with the crack of the bat. Jackie looked to see where the ball was before deciding if he should run past first base or make the turn and go to second.

The leftfielder still hadn't picked up the bouncing ball, so Jackie scooted on to second with a stand-up double. The Pasadena runner scored easily. The game was tied, 3–3.

The players on the Pasadena bench, who looked a little down before Jackie arrived, were suddenly on their feet. They were smiling, yelling, pounding each other on the back.

Jackie eventually came around to score, putting Pasadena ahead. They held the lead, thanks to another hit and a stolen base by Jackie. At the end of the game, the Pasadena Bulldogs were the Southern California Junior College Baseball Champions.

* * *

It had been a long day, and Jackie was bushed. When Ray dropped him off at Pepper Street around dinnertime, all he wanted to do was take a hot bath. As he walked up the front steps, Mack came out of the front door.

All afternoon Jackie had been worrying about what to say when he saw Mack. The two brothers were close, but they were competitive rivals too. Jackie didn't know how Mack would handle his little brother taking away his long jump record.

"I heard you had a pretty good day," Mack said. He wrapped his arms around Jackie and gave him a hug.

"You're not mad that I broke your record?" Jackie asked.

"If anybody was going to break it," Mack replied, "I'm glad that anybody was you. It keeps the record in the family, at least."

"Where are you heading?" Jackie asked.

US
OLYMPIC
TEAM
PASADENA

"I have to work tonight."

Jackie looked at Mack. His brother was wearing a pair of ripped old blue jeans and dirty T-shirt.

When Mack had returned from the 1936 Olympics, he didn't receive a hero's welcome. There was no parade through the streets of Pasadena in his honor. No commercial endorsements. No professional track and field tour. No job offers.

Mack took the only job he could find. He was a street sweeper for the city of Pasadena.

Even Jesse Owens, the world famous hero of the Olympics, wasn't much better off than Mack. Four gold medals didn't help him. He tried to turn his fame and incredible athletic ability into a career. He was reduced to putting on footrace exhibitions at state fairs to earn money. Sometimes he even raced against horses. But at least Jesse Owens wasn't picking up garbage off the streets to earn a living.

Jackie couldn't hide the disappointment in

his face when Mack pulled out his pushcart and broom. His brother was just twenty-four years old. Mack was one of the best athletes in the world, but the best days of his life were over. He had no opportunities. No chance for advancement. As a black man in America during the depression, he was lucky to have a job at all.

When Mack had returned from the 1936 Olympics, Jackie dreamed of making the Olympic team like his brother and competing in the 1940 Olympics. Not anymore. What was the point to it? So he could come home and become a street sweeper?

"It's not fair," Jackie said bitterly.

"I know," Mack replied with a shrug. "But what are you going to do?"

Mack pulled on his United States Olympic Team jacket and went out to sweep the streets of Pasadena.

I'm an Athlete

When Jackie graduated from Pasadena Junior College, he received offers from universities all around the country. They had heard about Jackie's heroics on the playing field, and they wanted him to play for their teams. Mallie Robinson couldn't afford to pay for a college education, but Jackie's skill in sports would allow him to attend the college of his choice for free.

After thinking it over, Jackie decided to enroll in the University of California at Los Angeles. The main reason he chose UCLA over all the other schools was that it was near his home. He would be able to stay close to his mother and family.

At UCLA, Jackie became a star. He was the first athlete in the university's history to earn varsity letters in four sports. He played shortstop for the baseball team. He was the basketball team's highest scorer. In football, he averaged twelve yards every time he carried the ball. That led the nation in yards per carry. He was the national long-jump champion in track and field.

Even though his brother Mack hadn't been able to turn his Olympic success into a career, Jackie thought about trying out for the Olympic track team. But he never got the chance. World War II had begun in Europe. The United States was not involved yet, but the 1940 Olympics were canceled.

Around that time something happened to Jackie Robinson that would change the course of his life.

28
18
UCLA
UCLA

Jackie was working part-time as a janitor at the UCLA student lounge. It was a big stone building called Kerckhoff Hall. He was sweeping up one day after class when he noticed a girl.

Jackie was shy with girls and didn't have a lot of time for a social life anyway. He had classes during the day, he played a sport every season, and he worked in the student lounge and the college bookstore.

Jackie didn't go out much at night, because he felt he had to be home and asleep by midnight to perform his best on the field the next day. On weekends he taught Sunday school at a local church. There wasn't a lot of time left over for girls.

But this girl was special. She was tall, with long hair and a friendly smile. She spent a lot of time in the student lounge, Jackie noticed. He found himself anxiously awaiting her arrival every day. He would go home disappointed if she didn't show up.

When she *did* show up, Jackie couldn't help but peek at her as he did his work. When the girl would glance anywhere in his direction, he would quickly look away.

Jackie's old friend Ray Bartlett also played football for UCLA, and one day he stopped into the student lounge to see Jackie.

"How come you keep looking over there?" Ray asked.

"I can't take my eyes off that girl," Jackie admitted.

"I know her," Ray informed Jackie. "Do you want me to introduce you?"

"No," Jackie said nervously. "I wouldn't know what to say."

"Oh, come on," Ray insisted, dragging Jackie across the student lounge. "Don't be silly."

The girl's name was Rachel Annetta Isum. Not only was she beautiful, but she was also a straight-A student. Rachel was a freshman, studying nursing.

"I'm Jackie Robinson," Jackie said awkwardly when Ray introduced him.

"I know," Rachel said. "The football player."

Before they met, Rachel imagined that Jackie was conceited and self-centered because he was such a good athlete. Jackie imagined that Rachel was probably quiet and dull because she was such a good student.

But judging people before you meet them usually leads to poor judgments. As it turned out, Rachel and Jackie were wrong about each other.

As Jackie walked her to the parking lot, he found Rachel to be warm and easygoing. Rachel found Jackie to be shy and gentlemanly. She liked his smile and his quiet confidence. He liked that she was direct, honest, and not afraid to disagree with him.

It wasn't long before Jackie and Rachel fell in love. Jackie knew that whatever he went through during the rest of his life, he would be going through it with Rachel at his side.

Rachel had just begun her college years, but Jackie's were winding down. One day in February 1940, Jackie sat her down and told her he had come to a big decision.

"I've given this a lot of thought," he told her. "I've decided to leave school."

"What?" Rachel was taken aback. "Are you joking, Jackie? You'll be graduating in a few months."

"No, I won't," Jackie announced seriously. "I want to get a job *now*. My mother has been supporting me all these years. She's getting older. It's time for me to start helping her."

"Why not get your college diploma first, and *then* get a job?" Rachel asked.

"What difference does it make?" Jackie said disgustedly. "I've seen black men with college diplomas. They're janitors. My brother Mack went to college. He's sweeping streets. No amount of education is going to help a Negro get a job."

Rachel looked sadly at Jackie. She had only

known him for a short time, but she already knew that once Jackie made up his mind, he wasn't likely to change it.

"I'm no scholar anyway, Rae," he said softly. "I'm an athlete."

But he was a *black* athlete. No amount of athletic ability was going to help him get a job in professional sports either.

If Jackie was white, he knew, a professional football team would sign him in a minute. If he was white, he could play major league baseball. The best he could hope for would be to land a job as a coach. Not a *head* coach. Not a manager. Those jobs all went to whites. He could be somebody's assistant.

Rachel tried to talk Jackie into staying in school long enough to get his degree, but it was no use. Four months before he would have graduated from college, Jackie Robinson left UCLA. His future was not rosy.

An Announcement

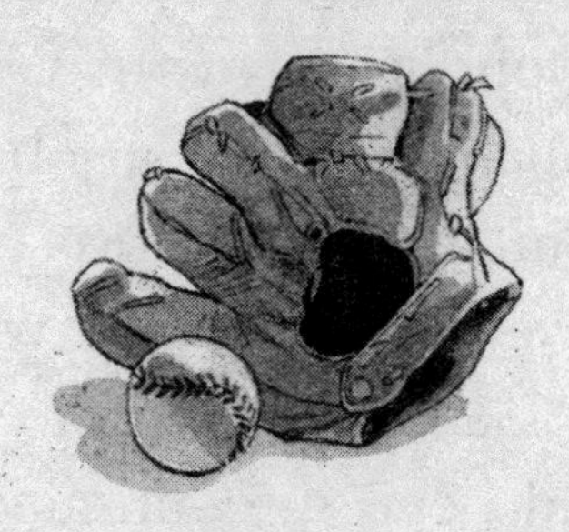

"Jackie," his mother, Mallie, called one morning in early 1941, "Who are the Honolulu Bears?"

"I don't know, Mom," Jackie replied. "Why?"

"There's a letter addressed to you from them."

Jackie tore open the envelope and learned that the Honolulu Bears were a semiprofessional football team based in Hawaii. They had heard about Jackie's passing and running at UCLA. They were interested in him joining the team. It didn't matter to the Bears that Jackie was black. The team had blacks, whites, and native Hawaiians on it.

Jackie thought it over. When he left UCLA, he had accepted a job through the National Youth Administration as an assistant athletic director working with kids in Atascadero, California. He loved it, but the program had been discontinued because of the war raging in Europe.

No other employers were knocking on Jackie's door. He always wanted to visit Hawaii. After talking it over with Rachel, Jackie accepted the offer from the Honolulu Bears.

Hawaii was not exactly the tropical paradise Jackie was expecting. The players on the Bears did not play a game once a week and then spend the rest of their time soaking up the sun on the beach. Part of the deal was that each player had to work on a construction crew all week and then play football on

Sunday. It was hard work. The pay was one hundred dollars a week. Good money, for 1941.

Jackie sparkled on the field, as usual, leading the Bears to many victories. But he missed Rachel, who was back home studying nursing at UCLA. He was anxious to get home, get a job, get married and start a family with Rachel.

Jackie was somewhat relieved when the Bears played their last game at the end of November. He booked passage on a ship called *Lurline* to take him home a week later.

December 7, 1941. The *Lurline* left Hawaii and was steaming toward Los Angeles. Jackie was on the forward deck playing cards with a few of his teammates.

Suddenly, members of the crew started rushing about. They were carrying big buckets of black paint and paintbrushes. One of them stopped at a window right next to the card game. Hurriedly, he dipped the brush into the bucket and painted over the window.

"What's going on?" Jackie asked the crew member before he moved on to the next window.

"Beats me," the crewman replied. "But I know it's not good. They told us to paint every window on the ship."

A few minutes later an announcement came over a loudspeaker telling everyone to gather on deck immediately. The captain waited until all had arrived before speaking.

"Attention!" he bellowed. "I have an important announcement to make. I just received word that Japan has launched a surprise attack on Pearl Harbor, the American naval base on the island of Oahu."

Gasps were heard from the people assembled on the deck. There had been a lot of talk about America entering World War II, but many people hoped that the country would be able to stay out of it. Everyone on the ship started buzzing.

“Attention!” the captain continued. “Most of the United States fleet was in that harbor. Nineteen of our ships were damaged or sunk in the attack. One hundred and eighty-eight of our planes were destroyed. They didn’t even have the chance to get off the ground. There were very few Japanese casualties. More than two thousand American soldiers were killed.”

A few people started sobbing.

“Are we at war?” someone called out.

“President Roosevelt is going to address the nation tomorrow,” the captain responded. “In the meantime we must travel carefully. These waters are very dangerous. This ship is not armed. We are vulnerable to attack from submarines, ships, and planes. Your windows are being painted black so that we can travel tonight without being seen. All lights on the deck will be turned off when the sun goes down. We will proceed to the mainland with as much caution as possible. Thank you, and

God bless the United States of America."

There was little sleep to be had by anyone on the *Lurline* that night. At any moment, everyone knew, a torpedo could slam into the hull and send the ship to the bottom of the Pacific.

As Jackie Robinson lay awake in his bunk, he thought about which direction life was going to take him. The president was certain to declare war on Japan the next day. Japan was an ally of Germany, so Hitler would probably declare war on the United States.

America would be right in the middle of World War II. As a twenty-two-year-old American man, it would be Jackie's duty to enlist in the armed forces and serve his country.

He had mixed feelings about that. He knew, of course, that Adolf Hitler was a racist and a dangerous dictator bent on taking over the world. Jackie was patriotic and loved his country.

But he also knew very well that black people in America were treated as inferior to whites by their own government. Why should he risk his life for a country that treated him and every other member of his race so poorly? Did he owe it to his country to fight for freedom, when he didn't have it at home?

In the end, Jackie Robinson did not have to decide what his course of action should be. Shortly after he got home to Pasadena, he received a letter in the mail. It wasn't an offer from the Honolulu Bears to play football next season. It was a draft notice from Uncle Sam. Jackie was to be a soldier in the United States Army.

The Army

When Jackie Robinson reported for duty at Fort Riley, Kansas, conditions for African-Americans were worse than he expected. The United States Army was segregated in 1942. Black Americans were fighting and dying for their country in the war, but they had to use separate bathrooms marked "Colored."

When the young soldiers weren't training for battle, they spent a lot of their free time playing sports. Rival teams from different forts would compete against one another. Shortly after Jackie arrived at Fort Riley, he went over to the baseball field and asked for a tryout.

The officer in charge of the baseball team looked Jackie over.

"You have to play for the colored team," the officer said.

Jackie watched the white players take batting practice for a minute or so, then turned and walked away slowly. He knew very well that there *was* no colored team.

While Jackie went through basic training in Kansas, Rachel remained in Los Angeles. During the day, she continued her nursing classes at UCLA. At night, she helped the war effort by working as a riveter at Lockheed Aircraft. Just about every day, Jackie would write her a long letter describing what he was going through. They both longed for the day when they could be together, get married, and raise a family.

At Fort Riley, Jackie was miserable. Even

without the racism, he would have been unhappy. He was training to become a member of the cavalry, which is the part of a military force that serves on horseback. Jackie didn't like riding horses.

But there was a way he could make his army experience better, Jackie realized. If he were an *officer*, he could get himself transferred out of Fort Riley. If he were an officer, soldiers would be forced to judge him by his rank instead of his skin color.

The army needed black officers, if only to command black troops. Jackie applied to Officer Candidate School and was accepted. After completing further training, he was promoted to second lieutenant.

Jackie was quickly transferred to the 761st tank battalion at Fort Hood, Texas. Things were better at Fort Hood. He didn't have to ride any horses. But he was involved in an incident that almost got him kicked out of the army.

The date was July 6, 1944. Jackie boarded a bus that shuttled soldiers from one end of Fort Hood to the other. He noticed a familiar face in the middle of the bus—Virginia Jones, the wife of one of his fellow officers. Jackie knew Virginia, and went over to sit next to her.

Virginia was an African-American like Jackie, but her skin was much lighter than his. To some people, she looked white. And a white woman sitting next to a black man on a bus was simply not allowed in 1944. Black men were sometimes *killed* if they were caught having anything to do with a white woman.

The bus driver glanced in his rearview mirror. He saw Jackie sit down next to what he thought was a white woman. Instantly, he stomped on the brake.

"Hey, you!" he shouted. "Move to the back of the bus!"

Jackie ignored him. He knew his rights.

The army had recently issued regulations barring racial discrimination on any vehicle operating on an army base.

The driver continued down the road, but when he saw that Jackie had not followed his order, he stomped on the brake again. This time, he got out of the driver's seat and went over to where Jackie was sitting.

"Get to the back of the bus where you colored people belong!" the driver insisted.

"I'll sit where I please," Jackie replied calmly, his arms folded defiantly across his chest.

(Years later, Rosa Parks would ignite the civil-rights movement when she refused to move to the back of a bus in Montgomery, Alabama. But this incident with Jackie Robinson took place eleven years before Rosa Parks.)

"If you don't move, boy," the driver warned, "you're gonna be in big trouble!"

Jackie didn't move.

The driver rushed off the bus and ran into a nearby building. Within minutes, sirens were sounded. A jeep arrived with two military policemen inside. The tires screeched to a halt in front of the bus. The policemen stormed on the bus and grabbed Jackie roughly by his arms.

"You're under arrest!" they said, pulling him up from his seat.

"What's the charge?" Jackie asked angrily.

"Drunk and disorderly."

Jackie had to laugh. When he was growing up, many of the teenagers on Pepper Street had experimented with alcohol. Some of them developed drinking problems. In his whole life Jackie had never had a drink. Not one.

But that didn't matter. The policemen hustled him out of the bus roughly and locked him up in the Fort Hood jail.

A military trial, called a court-martial, was held. If Jackie was convicted, he would be kicked out of the army and possibly do jail time also.

The bus driver told his side of the story. Jackie told his side of the story. The jury listened to many witnesses describe what happened on the bus that day. All of them—black and white—backed up Jackie's version of the way thing happened.

In the end Jackie was judged to be innocent of all charges.

After the incident on the bus, Jackie became disillusioned with the military. It had become clear to him that the army was as racist as the rest of America. When people looked at him, they didn't see an officer in the United States Army. They just saw a black man. His rank didn't matter. All that mattered was the color of his skin.

Jackie applied for his release from the military. In November 1944 he was given his honorable discharge.

Five months later Germany was defeated. Four months after that, atomic bombs were dropped on Japan. World War II was over.

After Jackie returned home to Pasadena, he wrote letters to dozens of colleges applying for a job as an athletic coach. He was supremely qualified. He had been a high school and college star athlete in four sports. He was a military veteran who had demonstrated leadership qualities in the army. He was young (twenty-five years old) and enthusiastic.

Three colleges responded to Jackie's letter with offers to come in for an interview. But mysteriously, whenever he showed up in person, nobody was interested in hiring him.

At the third college, the personnel secretary wouldn't even let Jackie in for his interview. After being forced to wait over an hour, he stormed out of the office and fumed in the hallway. An African-American janitor was sweeping up there.

"Are you okay, son?" he asked.

"I had an appointment for an interview with the personnel director," Jackie explained. "There's a job opening for a coach in the athletic department. Now they tell me the personnel director is in meetings all day."

"Did you make that appointment by phone?" asked the janitor.

"No, by mail."

"Did you happen to mention you were colored?"

Jackie shook his head no.

"Son," the janitor said, putting a hand on Jackie's shoulder. "You're wasting your time. They ain't gonna hire no colored coach."

Jackie looked at the janitor. Maybe he had the skills to be a coach. Maybe he wanted to be a doctor. Or even the president. Instead, he was a janitor. It was the same thing that had happened to Jackie's brother when he came home from the Olympics. The thought crossed Jackie's mind that despite his education, athletic ability, and military service, he too might end up sweeping floors.

Jackie walked away, feeling the same way he felt when he tried out for the army baseball team and was told to go play for the colored team.

Only this time, there *was* a colored team Jackie could play for.

Someone Is Watching

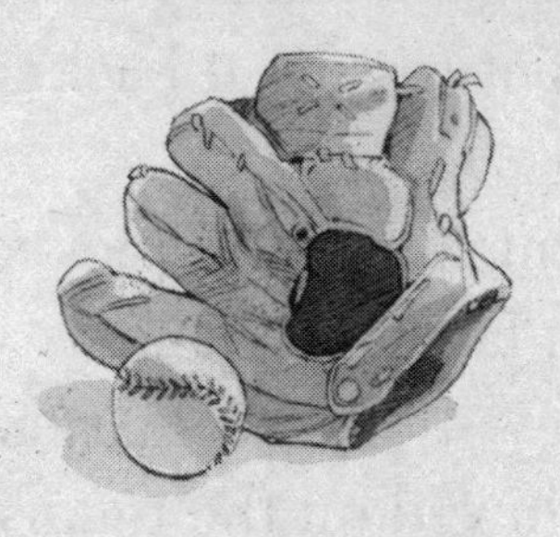

"Heads up!"

Jackie Robinson ducked and covered his head with his hands.

It was a few days before he would receive his official release from the army. Jackie was walking across a playing field near Camp Breckinridge in Kentucky. A second after he ducked and covered his head, a baseball flew inches from his ear and landed in the grass nearby.

"Sorry!" somebody in the distance yelled.

Jackie turned around to see who was yelling to him. A bunch of young black men were throwing and hitting baseballs around.

"How about tossing it back?" one of them hollered.

Jackie bent down and picked up the ball. He hadn't played any sports while he was in the army because African-Americans were not allowed on the teams. It had been several years since he had held a baseball in his hand.

Even so, it felt good. Jackie wrapped his fingers around the seams just as he did in his college days. He rifled the ball on a line to the player who had yelled to him.

"Nice arm," the player said after the ball smacked into his glove.

"Thanks," Jackie replied.

"You must be a ballplayer."

"I played in college," Jackie replied. "At UCLA. My name is Jackie Robinson."

"Yeah, I think I read something in the paper about you."

The player stuck out his hand and said his name was Hilton Smith. He was a pitcher, he said, and for the last eight years he had been playing for a team called the Kansas City Monarchs. It was a name Jackie knew well.

Because African-Americans had been banned from major league baseball, they had been forming their *own* teams as far back as 1862. The Negro Leagues—separate leagues composed entirely of African-American players—were very popular in the 1920s, 1930s, and 1940s.

The Kansas City Monarchs were the best team in the Negro American League. Over the years they would win seventeen pennants, thanks to superstars like Satchel Paige, Cool Papa Bell, and John Henry Lloyd. Years later, all of these men would be inducted into the Baseball Hall of Fame.

"The Monarchs are looking for good young

players," Hilton Smith told Jackie. "You look like you might be one."

Smith suggested that Jackie write to the owner of the Monarchs, J. L. Wilkinson. The next time he saw Wilkinson, Smith said, he would put in a good word for Jackie.

Jackie wasn't sure it was such a great idea. He didn't like the idea of segregated leagues, whether it was white players *or* black players. It just didn't seem right to him. Athletes should just be athletes, he felt. Skin color should have nothing to do with who plays on a team. Black and white athletes should play together.

But that was out of the question in 1945. Jackie thought about what Hilton Smith said. Playing in an all-black league would give him an opportunity that the white world had denied him.

It wasn't as if Jackie had a lot of options before him. Job offers were not exactly pouring in. He wrote a letter to the Kansas City Monarchs.

Jackie was surprised when he got a quick reply. The Monarchs knew all about him from his college days. They knew he was a great all-around athlete and felt confident that he could be successful in the Negro League.

And it just so happened that the Kansas City Monarchs were looking for a shortstop. Jackie wouldn't even have to try out.

Jackie and Rachel had a long talk about whether or not accepting the offer from the Monarchs would be a good decision. Playing baseball would take him away from home again. It would delay their marriage. But the pay would be 400 dollars a month. It was more money than Jackie had ever made. Maybe he could save some money.

Within days Jackie Robinson was on a train to Kansas City.

* * *

Jackie was a little concerned that his baseball skills would be rusty. It had been almost five years since his last game at UCLA.

He didn't have to worry. The army had made him bigger, stronger, tougher, and faster. At twenty-five he was a *better* ballplayer than he had been at twenty.

Jackie tore apart the Negro League, hitting .387. He terrorized opposing pitchers on the base paths and gobbled up every ball hit his way in the field. In the annual Negro League All-Star game, he represented the Monarchs.

Off the field, being a Negro League star was nothing like being a major league star. The Monarchs did not travel around by airplane and stay in fancy hotels. They rode from town to town on uncomfortable old buses that kept breaking down. They stopped at restaurants and hotels that would refuse to serve them because they were black. Sometimes the team ate and slept on the bus.

Some days the Monarchs would play a

morning game, then pile into the bus and drive a hundred miles for an afternoon game. Then, they would drive another hundred miles and play a game that night. A *triple*-header!

That was just the way it was in the Negro League. There was no reason to believe it would ever be different.

Another reason Jackie didn't enjoy his time in the Negro League was because he missed Rachel. She had graduated from UCLA and was working as a nurse at Los Angeles General Hospital. In long letters back and forth, they wrote about how happy they would be after they got married and started their family.

But neither of them could imagine that happening as long as Jackie was bumping around the country on a bus with the Monarchs.

* * *

Then one day late in the season, Jackie was

scooping up grounders on the infield before a game. His teammate Satchel Paige, who was one of the greatest pitchers in baseball history, strolled over to him.

"See that white guy in the stands on the third base side?" he asked Jackie.

"Yeah, I see him."

"He's been watching you, son."

"No way!" Jackie replied.

"That guy has been to our last three games. He always sits in the same place. He's always writing in a notebook. He must be a scout."

"A scout?" Jackie asked. "For who?"

"Could be the Brooklyn Dodgers," Paige replied. "I hear they're starting up a new black league. Could be the Cleveland Indians. Could be somebody else. You know *one* of them is gonna take a chance on one of us sooner or later. You can bet on that."

"If he's a scout, he's got to be watching you, Satch. You're the best there's ever been."

"No." Paige shook his head sadly. "They

think I'm too old. If they take a chance on one of us, they'll pick somebody young. Somebody who has a career ahead of him. Like you. I've been watching that guy. It's *you* he's looking at."

Something Wonderful

The white man in the stands *was* a scout. His name was Clyde Sukeforth, and he worked for the Brooklyn Dodgers. After the game he came down to the edge of the field and introduced himself to Jackie.

"Would you come to New York with me?" Sukeforth asked. "My boss wants to meet you."

"What for?" Jackie asked.

"I honestly don't know," Sukeforth admitted. "He wouldn't tell me."

"Let's go," Jackie said.

* * *

It was a very hot August day when Clyde Sukeforth escorted Jackie to 215 Montague Street in Brooklyn, New York. Sukeforth took Jackie up to the fourth floor. A sign on the big wooden door read:

BRANCH RICKEY

PRESIDENT, BROOKLYN DODGERS

Sukeforth knocked gently on the door, and then opened it. Behind a big mahogany desk sat a man who looked to be in his sixties. He wore thick glasses, and his bushy eyebrows almost seemed to rest on top of them. He had a cigar in his mouth. Despite the heat, he wore a rumpled jacket and tie.

"You must be Jackie Robinson," the man said, looking up. "I'm Branch Rickey."

Rickey stood up and extended his hand. He gestured for Jackie to sit on the big leather chair across the desk. As he sat down, Jackie glanced around the office. There was a fish

NCH
KEY
dent
klyn
gers

tank on one side of the room. On the opposite wall was a portrait of Abraham Lincoln. There were shelves and shelves of books.

Branch Rickey stared at Jackie for a long time before saying anything.

"Have you got a girl, Jackie?" he finally asked.

"Yes."

"Good. You're going to need her."

"Why?"

"Because there are times in a man's life when he needs a woman by his side."

Rickey leaned forward in his chair and fixed his gaze intently on Jackie's face. Jackie locked eyes with him.

"Do you know why I asked you to come here today?" Rickey asked in a deep, booming voice.

"The word is you're starting a new Negro league," Jackie replied. "They say you're recruiting players for a team called the Brown Dodgers."

Rickey let out a satisfied laugh.

"There are no Brown Dodgers, Jackie," he said, smiling. "I just made that up to keep my true intentions secret."

"So why *am* I here?" Jackie asked.

"For sixty years," Rickey continued, "my fellow team owners have refused to let qualified players of your race be a part of the national pastime. It has been racist and I feel disgusted to have been part of it. Your people fought and died in the war, and should have the right to do anything a white man in America can do. That includes play major league baseball, in my opinion."

Rickey took a deep breath before continuing.

"Jackie, I have decided to break down the color barrier. I'm looking for the right man to do it with me."

Jackie was speechless. He never thought the day would come when a black man would play in the major leagues. Even in his wildest dreams, he never imagined that *he* would be that man.

Rickey was just getting warmed up.

"For the past year, I have been on a secret worldwide manhunt," he said. "We have scouted Negro players in America, Cuba, Mexico, Puerto Rico, and Venezuela. I narrowed the list down to a few young men, and you're at the top of the list."

Jackie gulped. The importance of this meeting was beginning to sink in. If he accepted Rickey's offer, he would not simply be a baseball player. He would be representing his entire race. If he succeeded, all African-Americans would succeed with him. And if he failed, all African-Americans would fail with him. There would be an incredible weight on his shoulders.

"Look," Rickey said, gesturing to the portrait of Lincoln on the wall. "I'm not trying to free the slaves. I'm trying to win the National League pennant. We need good ballplayers. I think you can play in the major leagues. Do you have what it takes?"

Jackie paused a long time before responding.

"Yes," he answered firmly.

"I thought so," Rickey beamed.

"May I ask you a question?" Jackie asked.

"Of course."

"Why *me*? There are better black players than me, and they're right here in America. You didn't have to search the world. Josh Gibson has hit more home runs than Babe Ruth. My own teammate Satchel Paige is the greatest pitcher ever."

Rickey took off his jacket and rolled up his sleeves.

"You're right," he said. "But this isn't just about runs, hits, and errors, Jackie. I needed a great player, of course. But I also need a great man. I need a gentleman, like you. I need a young man who is college educated, like you. I need a man of impeccable character and dignity, like you. I know you're all those things, Jackie. What I *don't* know is whether or not you have the guts."

Jackie bristled. He had always been quick to get angry, and here was this white man suggesting he might be a coward.

"I have the guts, Mr. Rickey," he said.

"Are you sure?" Rickey said as he came around the desk to get face-to-face with Jackie. "What are you going to do when the team checks into a hotel and some white clerk behind the front desk says he won't give you a room because they don't admit blacks? Are you going to slug him?"

Rickey didn't wait for Jackie's answer. He just continued right on.

"What are you going to do when you're in a restaurant and a waiter calls you a nigger and refuses to serve you? Are you going to curse him out? What are you going to do when an opposing player slides into second base, spikes high, and cuts you and calls you a dirty so-and-so? Are you going to start a riot?"

Rickey was right in Jackie's face. He paused, then relaxed and sat on the edge of his desk. "Jackie, you know as well as I do that all these things and more are going to happen to the first man to break the color barrier. What are you going to do when the fans, the sportswriters, even the players on your own team *hate* you because of the color of your skin? Are you going to fight back?"

"Mr. Rickey," Jackie asked, "are you looking for a ballplayer who is afraid to fight back?"

"No," Rickey bellowed, "I'm looking for a ballplayer with guts enough *not* to fight back."

The two men stared at each other for a long time.

"Jackie, I have given this a lot of thought over the last year. "Only with nonviolence—by turning the other cheek—will you be able to open the door to integrate baseball, and all sports down the line. It's the only way. If the first black player is involved in a single incident, it might be another ten or twenty years before another Negro gets a chance. So I only want you on my team if you can hold your anger in check."

"Mr. Rickey," Jackie said seriously. "I'm a fighter. I fight back. All my life I have fought back. But no matter what happens to me, there will be no incidents. That's a promise."

"I knew you would say that," Rickey beamed. "It is precisely because you are a fighter that I chose you."

Rickey opened his desk drawer and pulled out a contract with Jackie's name on it. Today, professional athletes make millions of dollars each year. But back in the 1940s, they made much less money. Especially rookies. Jackie's contract called for him to receive a $3,500 bonus for signing and $600 a month. That was it.

Jackie accepted a pen from Rickey and signed the contract.

"One more thing," Rickey said as Jackie stood up. "I don't want word of this to get out until I'm ready to make a public announcement. I need you to keep it secret."

"May I tell my girlfriend?"

"Not yet."

It had been a long meeting. Jackie was exhausted, but exhilarated at the same time. That night, he called Rachel on the phone.

"Something wonderful happened today, Rae," he gushed. "It's going to affect both of us. I can't tell you about it right now. But you'll know soon enough."

The Barrier Comes Down

It was a cloudy, chilly day in Brooklyn on April 15, 1947. But Mallie, Mack, Edgar, Frank, and Willa Mae Robinson didn't mind. They had all piled into their 1936 Ford and driven all the way from California—to see a baseball game.

It wasn't any old baseball game. It was Opening Day. More importantly, it was the first Opening Day in sixty years in which an African-American player was to take the field alongside white players.

Jackie Robinson had spent the 1946 season playing for the Dodgers' top minor league team, the Montreal Royals. He had a phenomenal year. Jackie led the league in hitting (.349), runs scored (113), and fielding average for second basemen. He stole forty bases. The Royals won the pennant by eighteen games and also won the minor league World Series.

Off the field, it had also been a wonderful year. Just before the season started, Jackie and Rachel finally got married. When the season ended, their first child, Jackie Jr., was born.

Little Jackie Jr., just five months old, was in the stands on Opening Day, swaddled in a blanket. He didn't know what was going on around him. But the rest of the 26,623 people in Ebbets Field realized they were about to witness a historic moment.

In the Dodger dugout, Pee Wee Reese, Eddie Stanky, Carl Furillo, Dixie Walker, Pete

Reiser, and the other members of the team shuffled around to get rid of their nervous tension. Batboys scurried here and there, making sure all the equipment was ready.

In the stands vendors hawked hot dogs and peanuts. Late arriving fans hurried to their seats anxiously. There was a special anticipation felt by the many African-American fans in the ballpark.

"Ladies and gentlemen," the public address announcer boomed, "the 1947 Brooklyn Dodgers!"

Everyone stopped what they were doing. As a group, the Dodgers ran out of the dugout.

A few scattered boos were heard, but they were drowned out by thousands of people—black and white—cheering together.

Any decent human being had to agree that this was a moment that was fair, necessary, and long overdue.

When Jackie Robinson stepped across the

foul line and took his position at first base, the color barrier was broken.

* * *

Jackie Robinson didn't do anything spectacular that day. In fact, he went hitless. At the start of the season, he was nervous and tight. He was trying too hard. He wanted to prove himself so badly.

That rookie season was probably the toughest season any baseball player ever had to endure. Wherever the Dodgers went, some fans booed Jackie and cursed him. Many hotels and restaurants refused to serve him. Several opposing teams threatened to walk off the field if Jackie walked on it. Some of his own teammates did not want to play with Jackie. A few asked to be traded. Every day nasty letters arrived in the mail, some with death threats against Jackie and his family.

On several occasions Jackie thought about quitting. But he was very strong and determined. No matter what anybody said or did to him, he refused to give up. And he kept his promise to Branch Rickey that he would not fight back.

Despite all the pressure he was under, Jackie was able to settle down and play baseball the way he knew how. He started hitting the ball and creating havoc on the base paths. He went on a twenty-one-game hitting streak. On June 24 he stole home for the first of many times. The same month he scored all the way from first base on a sacrifice fly.

When Jackie got on base, everybody in the ballpark stopped to watch him. They knew he would steal a base, rattle the pitcher, or do *something* to set up a rally for the Dodgers. People said he was the most exciting thing to happen to baseball since Babe Ruth.

As the 1947 season went on, Jackie won the respect of his teammates, opposing players, baseball fans, and people all over the country. He was on the cover of *Time* magazine. A poll named him the second most respected man in the United States (singer Bing Crosby came in first). He won the Rookie of the Year Award.

When the season ended, Jackie led the league in stolen bases. He led the Dodgers in runs, singles, bunt hits, total bases, stolen bases, and tied for the team lead in doubles and homers. And the Dodgers won the pennant, just as Branch Rickey hoped they would when he signed Jackie.

After that breakthrough season, Jackie Robinson went on to a great career with the Brooklyn Dodgers. His best season was 1949, when he led the National League in batting and stolen bases. He also was voted the Most Valuable Player in the league.

In Jackie's ten years with the Dodgers, he led them to six pennants. Five times they were defeated by the New York Yankees in the World Series. Finally, in 1955, the Dodgers beat the Yankees to win their first

and only World Series. Three years later the team moved to Los Angeles and became the Los Angeles Dodgers.

After the 1956 season, Jackie retired from baseball. By that time there were many African-American players. Other sports opened their doors to African-American players also.

Imagine what sports would be like in the second half of the twentieth century without athletes such as Hank Aaron, Willie Mays, Ken Griffey Jr., Jim Brown, Walter Payton, Wilt Chamberlain, Shaquille O'Neal, Michael Jordan, and so many others. Jackie Robinson blazed the trail for all of them to follow.

Everything Is Complete

It was a cloudy day in Cooperstown, New York, on Monday, July 23, 1962. But the weather didn't bother Jackie Robinson. Nothing could bother Jackie on this day. Because this was the day he would be inducted into the National Baseball Hall of Fame.

Thousands of people gathered for this very special occasion in the little town in upstate New York. Jackie's family and friends. His former teammates. Players who played against him. Fans from all over the country gathered to honor the man who broke baseball's color barrier and changed the world in the process.

To be eligible to enter the Baseball Hall of Fame, a player must be retired for five years. Most of the members of the Hall of Fame had to wait many, many years before they were voted in. In 1962 nobody had ever been voted into the Hall of Fame the first year they were eligible. Even the great Joe DiMaggio had to wait several years before he made it. Jackie Robinson was the first player ever to be chosen the first year he was eligible.

As Jackie mounted the podium to the cheering of the crowd, his plaque was unveiled for all to see. The face on the plaque wasn't black, or white. It was bronze, like all the other members of the Hall of Fame. The words on the plaque did not say Jackie was a black man. It didn't say that qualified players with his skin color were barred from playing in the major leagues for sixty years. It didn't discuss the hardships he had to endure, being the first man of his race to crash through the color barrier.

If you visit the National Baseball Hall of Fame, you can see that plaque. It reads very simply:

LEADING N.L. BATTER IN 1949. HOLDS FIELDING MARK FOR SECOND BASEMAN PLAYING IN 150 OR MORE GAMES WITH .992. LED N.L. IN STOLEN BASES IN 1947 AND 1949. MOST VALUABLE PLAYER IN 1949. LIFETIME BATTING AVERAGE .311. JOINT RECORD HOLDER FOR MOST DOUBLE PLAYS BY SECOND BASEMAN, 137 IN 1951. LED SECOND BASEMEN IN DOUBLE PLAYS 1949–50–51–52.

That's it. All Jackie's life he had struggled to be treated like any other human being. Finally, that dream had come true.

Jackie had to wait a long time until the applause died down. When it did, he cleared his throat and began to speak. He gave thanks to the three people who had made it possible for him to be there that day. First, his mother, Mallie, who had showed him the quiet dignity he would later need. Second, his wife, Rachel, who had helped him endure the pressure and the pain that came from accomplishing what he did. Finally, he thanked Branch Rickey, who had the courage to break down the color barrier when all the other men who ran baseball were happy to keep things the way they were. All three—Mallie Robinson, Rachel Robinson, and Branch Rickey—were there to witness the historic event.

"I gave baseball all I had for ten years," Jackie Robinson told the crowd, "and baseball has given me everything I've got today. I can only say that now everything is complete."

Once again, the crowd erupted into cheers. The cheering came not just from those assembled in Cooperstown. President

John F. Kennedy sent this message about Jackie Robinson:

He has demonstrated in his brilliant career that courage, talent and perseverance can overcome the forces of intolerance. The vigor and fierce competitive spirit that characterized his performance as an athlete are still evident in his efforts in the great battle to achieve equality of opportunity for all people.

Martin Luther King sent this message about Jackie Robinson:

Back in the days when integration wasn't fashionable, he underwent the trauma and the humiliation and the loneliness which comes with being a pilgrim walking the lonesome byways toward the high road of Freedom. He was a sit-inner before sit-ins, a freedom rider before freedom rides.

Now that he was one of baseball's "immortals," it would have been easy for Jackie Robinson to retire to a life of leisure. He was famous and had a nice home in a beautiful neighborhood in Connecticut. He could have made lots of money just by signing his name on baseball memorabilia. But he didn't.

Even though Jackie was treated respectfully as a famous celebrity wherever he went, he was well aware that ordinary black citizens didn't receive that same treatment. There was still a lot of prejudice in the world. Job discrimination. Housing discrimination. Blacks still were not allowed to enter many schools, hospitals, restaurants, hotels, and country clubs. African-Americans still had to deal with prejudice every day of their lives.

This was not some foreign dictatorship hundreds of years ago. It was the United States of America, in the 1960s.

Jackie Robinson realized that he could use his fame to make the world a better place. He decided to devote the rest of his life to making things fair for all Americans. He led marches for civil rights. He put pressure on elected politicians to change unfair laws. He organized Athletes for Juvenile Decency. He spoke his mind on a radio program, and wrote his opinions in a newspaper column. He was a tireless speaker, spreading the word at graduations, dinners, anywhere groups of people gathered.

Jackie Robinson was forty-three years old on the day he was inducted into the National Baseball Hall of Fame. But his hair was blanketed in gray and he looked a lot older than his years. Few people knew that Jackie was already suffering from the disease that would eventually kill him.

Shortly after his baseball career came to an end, Jackie was diagnosed with diabetes. It's a disease in which the body does not produce enough of an important hormone called insulin. To fight the disease, he had to give up his beloved ice cream and desserts. He also had to inject himself with insulin every day to regulate his blood sugar level.

By taking good care of himself, he was able to control his diabetes for a long time. But eventually, the disease got the better of him. He went blind in one eye. The legs that terrorized pitchers on the base paths could barely walk. Ten years after he entered the Baseball Hall of Fame, he died. Jackie Robinson was just fifty-three years old.

The Impact of Jackie Robinson

Jackie Robinson's childhood home on Pepper Street in Pasadena was torn down long ago. But where that house stood is a plaque that reads simply: "Jackie Robinson resided on this Site with his Family From 1922 to 1946."

Nearby, a park where Jackie used to play is now called Jackie Robinson Park. The Jackie Robinson Community Center is in Pasadena too. The baseball stadium at UCLA where Jackie used to play is named after him as well.

All over the United States are streets, playgrounds, and community centers named in honor of Jackie Robinson.

But Jackie's impact goes way beyond plaques and signs with his name on them. He was truly one of the most important Americans of the twentieth century.

When Jackie Robinson broke through the color barrier in 1947, schools were strictly segregated in some parts of America. Sports were segregated. The military was segregated. Restaurants, hotels, and even drinking fountains were segregated. America was a segregated country.

Martin Luther King Jr. was just a teenager in 1947. Until King became a national figure, Jackie Robinson was the symbol for civil rights and racial integration in America.

When people—black and white—saw the quiet dignity, courage, and fierce determination Jackie displayed on the field despite the pressure he was under, they changed their attitudes.

White people came to realize that if Jackie Robinson could play major league baseball, there was really no difference between black people and white people other than the color of their skin. Black people came to realize that if Jackie Robinson could play major league baseball, it would be possible for *them* to set whatever goals they wanted and to achieve them.

Jackie Robinson played a major role in changing our country from one in which an entire race of people were treated as inferior. He inspired two generations of children—your parents and grandparents—to fight for what they believe in.

And it all started with a simple philosophy Jackie learned from his mother, Mallie: Doing good brings good. The best way to fight back is to show how *good* you are. If you prove yourself, people will drop their prejudice against you. They will come to respect and admire you, no matter what color skin you happen to have or country you happen to come from.

There is still prejudice in the world. A lot of it. But Jackie Robinson made things a lot better. For everyone.

A Jackie Robinson Chronology

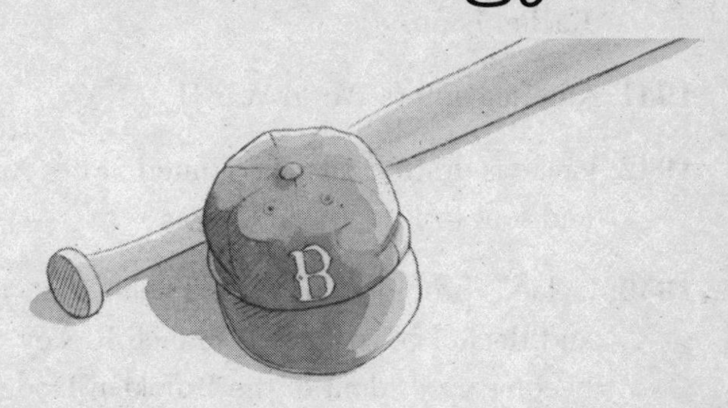

1909: Jackie Robinson's parents, Mallie and Jerry Robinson, get married.

1919: Jackie Robinson is born on January 31.

1924: Jackie enters Grover Cleveland Elementary School.

1926: Jackie enters Washington Elementary School.

1931: Jackie enters George Washington Junior High.

1935: Jackie enters John Muir Technical High School.

1936: Jackie's brother Mack wins two medals in track at the Summer Olympics.

1937: Jackie enters Pasadena Junior College.

1939: Jackie enters UCLA.

1940: Jackie is introduced to UCLA freshman Rachel Isum.

1941: America enters World War II.

1942: Jackie is drafted into the United States Army and sent to Fort Riley, Kansas.

1943: Jackie is promoted to second lieutenant. He and Rachel get engaged. Branch Rickey becomes president of the Brooklyn Dodgers.

1944: Jackie is transferred to Fort Hood, Texas. He receives an honorable discharge from the army.

1945: World War II ends. Jackie plays for the Kansas City Monarchs of the Negro League. He meets with Branch Rickey and signs a contract with the Brooklyn Dodger organization.

1946: Jackie plays for the Montreal Royals, an AAA team. He and Rachel are married on February 10. Their first child, Jackie Jr., is born on November 18.

1947: Jackie plays his first game for the Brooklyn Dodgers on April 15. He wins the first Rookie of the Year award. The New York Yankees beat the Dodgers to win the World Series.

1948: President Harry S Truman orders that segregation be eliminated from American armed forces and federal workplaces.

1949: Jackie has his best year. He leads the National League in hitting and wins the Most Valuable Player Award. The Yankees beat the Dodgers in the World Series again.

1950: Daughter Sharon Robinson is born on January 13.

1952: Son David Robinson is born on May 14. The Yankees beat the Dodgers in the World Series again.

1953: The Yankees beat the Dodgers in the World Series again.

1954: The United States Supreme Court orders that segregation be eliminated in schools.

1955: The Brooklyn Dodgers win their first and only World Series.

1956: The Yankees beat the Dodgers in the World Series again.

1957: Jackie retires from baseball. He begins a new career as a businessman, civil-rights activist, journalist, and radio commentator.

1958: The Brooklyn Dodgers move to Los Angeles.

1962: Jackie is inducted into the National Baseball Hall of Fame.

1965: Branch Rickey dies at the age of eighty-four.

1972: Jackie Robinson dies at the age of fifty-three on October 24.

1984: Jackie is awarded the Medal of Freedom, which is awarded by the United States government to citizens who have performed positive acts or service to the country.

1997: The fiftieth anniversary of Jackie Robinson breaking the color barrier. Major league baseball retires his number 42 forever.

Appendix

John Roosevelt "Jackie" Robinson
Born January 31, 1919, at Cairo, GA.
Died October 24, 1972, in Stamford, CT.
5'11 1/2", 195 lbs.,
batted right, threw right

Career Statistics

Year	Club	League	Pos	G	AB	R	H	2B	3B	HR	RBI	SB	BA
1945	Kansas City	NAL	SS	47	163	36	63	14	4	5	23	13	.387
1946	Montreal	INT	2B	124	444	113	155	25	8	3	66	40	.349
1947	Brooklyn	NL	1B	151	590	125	175	31	5	12	48	29	.297
1948	Brooklyn	NL	2B/1B/3B	147	574	108	170	38	8	12	85	22	.296
1949	Brooklyn	NL	2B	156	593	122	203	38	12	16	124	37	.342
1950	Brooklyn	NL	2B	144	518	99	170	39	4	14	81	12	.328
1951	Brooklyn	NL	2B	153	548	106	185	33	7	19	88	25	.338
1952	Brooklyn	NL	2B	149	510	104	157	17	3	19	75	24	.308
1953	Brooklyn	NL	INF/OF	136	484	109	159	34	7	12	95	17	.329
1954	Brooklyn	NL	INF/OF	124	386	62	120	22	4	15	59	7	.311
1955	Brooklyn	NL	INF/OF	105	317	51	81	6	2	8	36	12	.256
1956	Brooklyn	NL	INF/OF	117	357	61	98	15	2	10	43	12	.275
	Major League Totals			1382	4877	947	1518	273	54	137	734	197	.311

World Series Record

Year	Club	League	Pos	G	AB	R	H	2B	3B	HR	RBI	BA
1947	Brooklyn	NL	1B	7	27	3	7	2	0	0	3	.259
1948	Brooklyn	NL	2B	5	16	2	3	1	0	0	2	.188
1952	Brooklyn	NL	2B	7	23	4	4	0	0	1	2	.174
1953	Brooklyn	NL	OF	6	25	3	8	2	0	0	2	.320
1955	Brooklyn	NL	3B	6	22	5	4	1	1	0	1	.182
1956	Brooklyn	NL	3B	7	24	5	6	1	0	1	2	.250
	World Series Totals			38	137	22	32	7	1	2	12	.234

Career Highlights

Led National League in stolen bases (39) 1947 and (37) 1949; hit for cycle (first game) August 29, 1948; led second basement in double plays 1949 through 1952.

World Series Records—Tied record for assists by second baseman in one inning (3); seventh inning, October 8, 1949; tied for mark by getting four bases on balls in a game October 5, 1952. One of 12 players to steal home in a World Series game, accomplishing fear in first game, eighth inning, September 28, 1955.

Named by *The Sporting News* as Rookie of the Year, 1947.
Named as second baseman on *The Sporting News* All-Star Major League Team, 1949–50–51–52.
Named Most Valuable Player, National League, 1949.
Named to Hall of Fame, 1962.

From the Jackie Robinson Reader

Follow the 

on their quest for the championship in the action-packed new baseball series from Aladdin Paperbacks and Atheneum Books for Young Readers.

Simon & Schuster Children's Publishing Division

Simon & Schuster Children's Publishing Division

Don't miss these other great baseball titles from Aladdin Paperbacks!

Heroes of the Game: True Baseball Stories
by Terry Egan, Stan Friedman, and
Mike Levine
(0-689-81352-X $4.50 US, $5.99 CA
True stories about the successes a
trials of major stars, average playe
and even baseball fans.

How to Snag Major League Baseballs: More Than 100 Tested Tricks That Really Work
by Zack Hample
(0-689-82331-2 $3.99 US, $5.50 CAN)
Learn how to bring home the ultimate souvenir from a game by someone who ought to know—he's snagged over 1,000 major league balls!

Simon & Schuster Children's Publishing Division
where imaginations meet
www.SimonSaysKids.com

Pitchers by George Sullivan
(0-689-82454-8 $7.99 US, $11.50 CAN)
Read about twenty-seven of the most famous pitchers in the history of baseball.

Sluggers by George Sullivan
689-82455-6 $7.99 US, $11.50 CAN)
A look at twenty-seven famous sluggers who have brought excitement to the game.

McGwire & Sosa: A Season to Remember
by James Preller
(0-689-82871-3 $5.99 US, $8.50 CAN)
Read about the magical season of '98, when Sammy and Mac became a part of baseball history.